Editorial

From Hiroshima to Fukushima

Hiroshima means 'wide island' The tidal rivers of the delta dissect the modern city, which has grown beyond its initial island location. It is a rather beautiful situation, surrounded by green, wooded hills. In August, the sun beats down on covered heads of those many thousands of people hurrying to gather at the Hiroshima Peace Memorial to remember the 275,000 victims of 'Little Boy', the uranium bomb dropped by Enola Gay, as the US Air Force had dubbed, respectively, their weapon of mass destruction and the plane that delivered it.

The nuclear explosion was detonated some 600 metres above Hiroshima at 8.15 on 6 August 1945, a virtually cloud-free Monday morning. Apparently, the city was chosen from three possible targets, not least because weather conditions were 'ideal' for the assault. A clear sky also assisted shooting the photographic record of this, the first of two experimental detonations. The second, over Nagasaki three days later, was a plutonium bomb, dubbed 'Fat Man', enabling comparisons to be drawn with the efficacy of the earlier uranium bomb dropped on Hiroshima. The city of Kokura was, in fact, the primary target on that Thursday morning, but it was obscured by smoke; so it was that Nagasaki, the secondary target, was bombed at 11.02 on 9 August.

It is 66 years since those terrible experiments, which instantly killed hundreds of thousands of people, many of them civilians. Tens of thousands more suffered lingering deaths due to their injuries, caused by intense heat, blast, and radiation sickness. Since that summer, no military or political leader has dared sanction the actual use of such a weapon of mass destruction, quite literally, although some have threatened their use at times of acute tension. Perhaps it was such uselessness that Earl Mountbatten had in mind when he remarked, in 1979, that

> 'As a military man who has given half a century of active Service I say in all sincerity that the nuclear arms race has no military purpose. Wars cannot be fought with nuclear weapons. Their existence only adds to our perils because of the illusions which they have generated.'

Such illusions are rather clearly perceived in Hiroshima, Nagasaki, and elsewhere in Japan. Indeed, as the nuclear disaster at Fukushima continues to unfold, Japanese perceptions have probed more deeply. Sumiteru Taniguchi survived extensive injuries suffered during the nuclear bombing of Nagasaki and, at 82 years of age, maintains a lively presence on behalf

Leabharlanna Fhine Gall

◄ *Visitors to the Hiroshima Peace Memorial Musum* (photo: Malaya Fabros).

of the Nagasaki Council of A-Bomb Sufferers (or *Hibakusha*, in Japanese). He recently observed that

> 'Nuclear power and mankind cannot co-exist. We survivors of the atomic bomb have said this all along. And yet, the use of nuclear power was camouflaged as "peaceful" and continued to progress. You never know when there's going to be a natural disaster. You can never say that there will never be a nuclear accident.'

There is a rising tide of opposition to nuclear power in Japan. Some mothers with young children are literally upping sticks and moving away from the region around Fukushima in an attempt to protect their children from the radioactive contamination which issues from the stricken plant.

The then Prime Minister, Naoto Kan, (he has since resigned), told this year's Hiroshima Peace Memorial Ceremony that Japan was 'starting from scratch' on energy policy, and that he regretted believing the 'safety myth' about nuclear power. Two-thirds of the country's nuclear power stations are switched off. Nuclear energy usually accounts for 30 per cent of energy needs, and this was projected to rise to 50 per cent by 2030. That would require 14 new reactors, in addition to the 54 already there. Of course, six of these at Fukushima are already failing, four of them in the most extreme fashion.

In response to all this, something is moving in Japan. It was reflected in this year's World Conference Against Atomic and Hydrogen Bombs, which we report in this issue of *The Spokesman*. The organisers remarked on the large numbers of new participants, many of them young people. Many such activists are also to be found supporting the encampments springing up in cities large and small around the world, in the wake of Occupy Wall Street. Something moves in our world.

Tony Simpson

*   *   *

All 544 first and second year students and eight teachers of the Hiroshima ➤
Municipal Girl's High School perished on the fine clear morning of 6 August 1945. They were engaged in demolition work close to the school, which was 500 metres from the hypocentre of the nuclear explosion. When students mobilized at other places in the city are included, the school lost 679 people, the most of any school in Hiroshima. The figure of the girl engraved in the centre of the monument carries a box carved with Einstein's formula $E=MC^2$. This indirect expression was a way around the occupying US army's prohibition on direct references to the 'atomic bombing'. Here, the site is carefully prepared for the 2011 commemoration ceremony. (Photo: Dave Webb, CND).

Hibakusha and Fukushima

Terumi Tanaka

I was 13 years old when an atomic bomb was dropped on Nagasaki, on 9 August 1945. At the time, I was reading a book on the second floor of my house, which was 3.2 km from the epicentre. The bomb killed five of my relatives. Although I have endured various kinds of suffering, I have managed to live to this day. Today, with other *Hibakusha* around the country, I am fighting together for a world free of nuclear weapons and for state compensation for A-bomb survivors.

On 11 March, a great earthquake hit eastern Japan, causing a massive tsunami devastating many cities and towns on the Pacific coast. The tsunami-ruined cities reminded *Hibakusha* of the devastation of Hiroshima and Nagasaki, 66 years ago. We were shocked and saddened as we thought of people who lost their family members and homes, as well as those who were killed in the disaster.

At the time, all four reactors at the Tokyo Electric Power Company's Fukushima Daiichi nuclear power plant lost off-site power, which led to the disfunctioning of the cooling system. Over the next few days, several hydrogen explosions occurred, releasing radioactive materials into the atmosphere. They were carried far and wide by the wind to the Kanto region. Fall-out landed on the ground with rain contaminating vast areas.

Residents living near the crippled nuclear power plant and many other people in wider areas were left without the necessary information about radioactive elements spreading around the region. This is why I can say many people must have been exposed to radiation, or inhaled

The author helped found the Japan Confederation of Atomic and Hydrogen Bomb Sufferers' Organizations (Nihon Hidankyo).

◄ *Mr Tanaka with participants at the 2011 World Conference* (photo: Corazon Fabros).

radioactive materials resulting in internal radiation exposure.

This fact was long kept from public knowledge. The utility and the government must be condemned for withholding it. The government said, 'There are no immediate health risks'. Doctors and scientists repeatedly insisted there is nothing to worry about, and did not provide any details. This gave rise to a sense of distrust among the public.

We, *Hibakusha*, have never imagined a massive emergence of more *Hibakusha* in Japan, the only A-bombed country. We have long called for no more *Hibakusha* to be created as a result of the use of nuclear weapons. We have worked hard to develop the movement to this end. So I deeply regret that such a large number of radiation victims have again been created in this country.

Damage from radiation exposure at Fukushima Daiichi is not the same as that of the atomic bomb survivors of Hiroshima and Nagasaki. Unlike *Hibakusha* who were proximally exposed to initial radiation (mainly neutron radiation and gamma rays), those who were more distally exposed *Hibakusha*, or *Hibakusha* who entered Hiroshima or Nagasaki to rescue victims after the bomb explosion, were in a similar situation to the *Hibakusha* in Fukushima. Those *Hibakusha* may not suffer massive doses of radiation entailing serious acute symptoms.

However, due to damage to their genes, the distally exposed *Hibakusha* could suffer from diseases such as cancer in five or ten years, or even 30 years later. Sixty-six years after the A-bomb was dropped, damage from radiation exposure still torments *Hibakusha*. *Hibakusha* from the Fukushima nuclear accident also experience such risks. The government and the power plant operator, TEPCO, should have made known this fact at an early stage and explained how to reduce these risks, and how to realize this goal while at the same time decreasing negative impacts on our health caused by the changes in our lives. However, TEPCO and the government covered up the fact, and experts in the media did not provide appropriate explanations and advice to the public. They said it is important to protect children, who live longer than adults and are susceptible to radiation. However, explanation about how infants absorb radiation into their thyroid was inadequate. Also, inappropriate explanations about caesium contamination in playgrounds raised concerns among parents.

I feel deep sympathy for *Hibakusha* created by the Fukushima accident and other recent *Hibakusha* elsewhere, who are forced to endure the same pain that A-bomb *Hibakusha* and global *Hibakusha* went through. I thought I would like to share their suffering. This is why we started our efforts to hold TEPCO and the government accountable for what they have done, including spreading the safety myth and causing massive suffering to the public, and also to demand compensation for damage to lives, health, mind and livelihood.

A-bomb survivors were left without proper support for twelve years after the bomb was dropped in 1945. In order to avoid making their bitter experience useless, in April, *Nihon Hidankyo* called on the government, TEPCO and the Fukushima Prefectural Government to take the following measures: the immediate issuance of disaster-victim certificates and health books to record what the victims have done after March 11, and the introduction of medical check-ups twice a year. The costs should be paid by the government. For many years to come, the government should be responsible for the health of radiation victims. If they fail to do this, whatever the government says, people's distrust and fear will only increase.

This year marks the 55th anniversary of *Nihon Hidankyo,* and the 66th year since the atomic bombings of Hiroshima and Nagasaki. The ten-year gap between the two events is due to the US policy of concealing the damage caused by the A-bombings, and the failure of the Japanese government to provide the sufferers with proper support. Due to these cover-ups and negligence, people paid no attention to the *Hibakusha* during that period. They were neglected and isolated from the general public around the country, suffering from unknown A-bomb diseases, which took many of their lives.

When the United States carried out a hydrogen bomb test explosion at Bikini Atoll, on 1 March 1954, the crew of a Japanese tuna fishing boat were showered with nuclear fall-out. Mr. Kuboyama, the ship's radio operator, died. This touched off the movement against atomic and hydrogen bombs throughout Japan. Encouraged and supported by the movement against A and H Bombs, *Hibakusha* who had participated in the 2nd World Conference against A and H Bombs, in 1956, founded the Japan Confederation of A- and H-Bomb Sufferers' Organizations (Nihon Hidankyo).

With *Hibakusha* increasing their struggle in close co-operation with their supporters, the Act for Atomic Bomb Sufferers' Medical Care was enacted in 1957, and the Special Measures Act for Atomic Bomb Sufferers in 1968. As a result of our strenuous effort over the last 55 years, demanding that the government issue A-Bomb Victim Health Insurance to *Hibakusha,* and that it pay state compensation, including for A-bomb deaths, the government has now the legal duty to pay premiums for all the A-Bomb Victim Health Insurance holders. More than 90 per cent of

Hibakusha can get some sort of benefits.

The major problem that had been left out of the aid and relief for *Hibakusha* was recognition that they have diseases caused by A-bomb radiation exposure. There was a system to provide sufficient care if one has illnesses recognized as radiation-related. But in those days, the number of those recognized as having A-bomb-related diseases was just 2,000 out of 300,000 *Hibakusha*. Even though the government lost Ms. Matsuya Hideko's lawsuit in the supreme court, it tightened up the criteria for recognition, far from improving them.

A series of collective *Hibakusha* lawsuits have been effective in forcing the government to change its unjust policies. After filing a lawsuit in 2003, 306 plaintiffs at 17 district courts sought recognition of their illnesses as caused by the atomic bombings. They won lawsuits until August 2009, when *Hibakusha* and the government reached agreement on ending the collective lawsuits. They had the government twice improve the criteria for A-bomb disease recognition. In the last three years, the number of cases of *Hibakusha* being recognized as suffering from atomic bomb-related illnesses has increased to 7,000. This victory was made possible because the inhuman nature of the damage done by the atomic bombings was widely exposed, as well as the fact of internal radiation exposure caused by radioactive fall-out, and because the movement has won broad support from the general public aspiring for the elimination of nuclear weapons.

But the government still refuses to recognize the diseases and exposure that have duly been recognized by the court decisions. There is a wide gap in judgment between courts and the government. We will continue to demand that further improvements be made to the criteria to bridge the gap.

Given the fact that the government's policy is one of asking *Hibakusha* to endure their suffering, we cannot expect fundamental improvements in *Hibakusha* policy. We should win compensation for the dead, the pillar of state compensation, and replace it with new legislation that will make clear, in name and reality, that they are the victims born of war launched and carried out by the state. *Nihon Hidankyo* is determined to promote the campaign further. Without the support of the wide range of Japanese people, state compensation will not be realized. I often hear people say, 'That's impossible'. But I believe this is a problem not only for *Hibakusha*, but for the Japanese people in general. With these aspirations, we will fight on to win a victory with the support of as many people as possible.

Finally, let me speak about energy policy based on nuclear power. *Nihon Hidankyo* has great concerns over the use of nuclear energy for power generation, and has called for a shift away from energy policy dependent on nuclear power. The recent nuclear accident at the Fukushima Daiichi nuclear power plant produced a lot of radiation victims. Nevertheless, the utility and the government are unable to bring the accidents under control. They can neither deal with nor control spent nuclear fuel and nuclear waste. In concluding my report as a *Hibakusha*, I am pleased to tell you that we, the *Hibakusha*, have decided to demand that the government and all the power companies should break away from the energy policy based on nuclear power, stop building new nuclear power plants, and shut down and decommission existing nuclear reactors one by one.

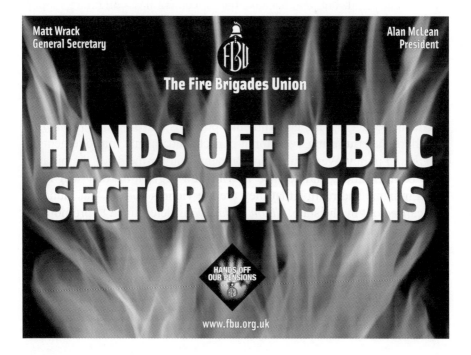

Fukushima's Quagmire

Hachiro Sato

*Mr Sato is a member if
Iitate Village Assembly in
Fukushima prefecture,
which is about 24 miles
north-west of the nuclear
disaster site.*

*He gave this address in
Hiroshima on 4 August
2011, during the World
Conference Against
Atomic and Hydrogen
Bombs.*

Let me begin by expressing our deepest gratitude to you for the warm support you have given us in goods and money, as well as in providing places to stay for the victims of the earthquake and the accident at the Fukushima Daiichi nuclear power plant.

The accident at Fukushima Daiichi is heading further into the quagmire, rather than coming under control. Right after it happened, about 120,000 people from Fukushima took refuge within or outside the prefecture. As of July 15 2011, this number has declined to 76,194, but the number of people who have fled from Fukushima prefecture has risen to 45,242, meaning 2.2 per cent of its population are forced to live elsewhere. One can only imagine the frustration and anxieties they live with every single day, having no idea about when they will be able to go back home. Those who continue to live in Fukushima, in places not designated as evacuation zones, are also deeply concerned: 'How many years can we live in such an environment where low levels of radiation continue to exist? Is it really true that there will be no ill-effects on our children?' No one has a clear-cut answer to these questions, and this is what concerns us most.

Administratively speaking, the village of Iitate, my hometown, became what it is today when it was merged with other neighbouring communities on 30 September 1956. Mountains and forests cover as much as 75 per cent of its 230 square-kilometre land area. It is a genuine farming community where our means of living are the production of rice, livestock, tobacco leaves, vegetables, flowers and

◀ *Dr Ishida of the Hiroshima Red Cross Hospital and A-Bomb Survivors' Hospital*
(photo: Malaya Fabros).

ornamental plants. 30.4% of our 6,170 inhabitants are old people, over 65 years old. The average yearly temperature is 10 degrees Celsius and the mean annual rainfall is about 1,300 millimetres. We have a cold climate in which the cold and wet easterly/northeasterly winds drift down during the early summer days. This, coupled with the late frost that comes as late as mid-May, damages our crops. We don't have much snowfall in winter, but the temperature can fall as low as 15 degrees Celsius below zero.

In spite of these unfavourable conditions, our ancestors and we have taken much pains and made great efforts in building the community. Today, Iitate has been chosen as one of 'Japan's most beautiful villages'. This year, 2011, was to have seen a leap of progress with the building of more factories and making local specialties for sale.

On 12 March, hydrogen explosions occurred at the No.1 and No. 3 reactors of the Tokyo Electricity Power Company's (TEPCO) Fukushima Daiichi nuclear power plant, followed later by fires at the No. 4 reactor, and partial destruction of the containment vessel of the No.2 reactor. These critical man-made disasters caused highly radioactive materials to fly in all directions and to spread over vast areas, including our village. All our villagers were forced to evacuate their homes, leaving everything behind including land, property, livelihoods and even hopes.

The need now is for the evacuees to prepare to return to the village and rebuild the infrastructure so that their health and safety will be ensured as well as the right to live. But the government, utility, prefectural and local administrations are too slow in carrying out measures in response to these needs. All this makes things even more difficult, along with the lack of credible information. For four months, since the start of the present disaster, the government and the utility have withheld important information. They have lied about what has happened, and even underestimated the present dangers. In the early stages, we accepted evacuees from Minami-soma City and Futaba Town. We assisted evacuees until March 18. It is regrettable that we supplied water and food contaminated with radioactive materials. On March 22, we learned from media reports that radioactive materials were detected in broccoli. Since then, radiation levels were announced every other day for milk, water and soil. Infants, pregnant women, children, young people and women were advised to leave the village voluntarily. Families were broken up, and people were forced to live in different evacuation centres.

The village authorities did not order all residents to leave their homes to fulfil their administrative responsibility. Instead, they requested the government to take special measures and carry out decontamination of firms and long-term nursing homes, which the village wanted to keep until the government designates their areas as exclusion zones. Many villagers began to voice angrily their rejection of nuclear power plants in their village. They did not know what to do in the present situation. Despite growing uncertainty, village mayor Sugeno Norio submitted a proposal to the central government, saying that the village had no intention of becoming an anti-nuclear flag-bearer.

Eight business establishments and a long-term nursing home continue to operate in the village. More than 800 villagers, including a 370-member 'security team' working three shifts to protect the village and its assets, have returned to the village. This is what's happening in our village. Isn't this the way to turn the people into guinea pigs to study the effects of low-level radiation exposure? We simply want no more nuclear power plants anywhere, whether they are in Fukushima, Japan or elsewhere in the world.

Our village has hosted nuclear power plants in the name of 'national policy' by accepting what the government explained as 'the use of nuclear energy for peaceful purposes'. No one imagined that a level 7 nuclear disaster would wipe out towns and villages, and displace large numbers of people to unknown places, where they would be unable to foresee what would become of them. The accident exposed the brutal outcome of over-optimistic views about Fukushima and on the part of national governments, which have believed the 'safety myth'.

Another factor that delayed an evacuation order was the lack of sufficient radiation monitoring sites in the prefecture, which hosts ten nuclear power plants! Right up to the disaster, there were only 23 monitoring posts within 20 kilometres, and only one near the prefectural government building, all under the control of the Local Development and Promotion Bureau. Regarding the prompt distribution of accurate information, what TEPCO and the Ministry of Trade, Economy and Industry are doing has been contrary to that which is needed. They have withheld needed information. Their underestimation of the crisis appears to be intentional. Fukushima residents are sick and tired of the comments they continue to make on television. To date, they refuse to admit that the nuclear accident is man-made.

In areas that are not designated as exclusion zones, parents are desperate to protect their children from radiation exposure. They are not sure if the one millisievert per year safety limit is really appropriate for the protection of children's health. They are confused by mixed and various kinds of information they see on the internet. We must seek to use the power of collective wisdom from around the world in order to save our children. To this end, we call for an authoritative independent body to be established.

The Fukushima Joint Centre for Post-disaster Reconstruction, which Fukushima Gensuikyo is working with, conducted an opinion survey on nuclear power plants. It shows 84.5 per cent of respondents favouring the decommissioning of all nuclear plants in Fukushima, and 79.3 per cent wanted TEPCO to compensate for the damage. One respondent said:

> 'The Fukushima Prefectural Government shouldn't allow TEPCO to take charge of disaster management at its power plant because it's just like asking a robber to look after your house.'

Another respondent said,

> 'Do you understand how painful it is to hear your child say he would die of cancer? We want safety to be restored in Fukushima!'

One more said:

> 'We need absolutely safe energy sources in place at any cost.'

Outrage and demands spilled out of the respondents' comments.

Following the nuclear disaster at Fukushima Daiichi, Italy and Germany decided to shut down their power plants. In Fukushima, the governor, Sato Yuhei, publicly reversed his position in the Fukushima Prefectural Assembly session of June 27. He said that Fukushima Prefecture should seek to build a community that does not depend on nuclear energy.

The Fukushima Prefectural Liaison Council for the Safety of Nuclear Power Plants, which consists of the prefecture's democratic organizations, has, for 38 years, been active in pointing out the danger of nuclear power plants, but neither the Fukushima prefectural government nor TEPCO has listened. They should have realized the danger before we had to go through such ordeals. Living in the only country to have been attacked with nuclear weapons, we should also have realized the precariousness of so-called 'atoms for peace'. To begin with, was it appropriate to regard what used to be weapons as safe? The fact is that we have no scientific method for the safe storage of spent fuels. Clearly, humankind cannot coexist with what is 'nuclear'. I believe it is our duty to work for the swift development of renewable energy sources in order to leave a safe and sound world for our children. We must call for no more nuclear victims.

Fukushima's Radioactive Elements

Helen Caldicott

Dr Caldicott has devoted much of her life to an international campaign to inform the public about the medical hazards of the nuclear age and the necessary changes in human behaviour to stop environmental destruction. Her most recent book is a revised and updated edition of If You Love This Planet *(W.W.Norton & Co.)*

Huge quantities of radioactive elements, more than anyone has been able or willing to measure, have been continuously released into the air and water since the multiple meltdowns at the Fukushima Daiichi Complex in Japan on and around 11 March 2011.

This accident is enormous in its medical implications. It will induce an epidemic of cancer the likes of which the world has only rarely experienced, as people inhale the radioactive elements, eat radioactive vegetables, rice and meat, and drink radioactive milk and teas.

As radiation from ocean contamination bio-accumulates up the food chain, radioactive fish will be caught thousands of miles from Japanese shores. As they are consumed, they will continue the cycle of contamination, proving that no matter where you are, all major nuclear accidents become local.

In 1986, a single meltdown and explosion at Chernobyl covered 40% of the European landmass with radioactive elements. Already, according to a 2010 report published by the New York Academy of Sciences, almost one million people have perished as a direct result of this catastrophe, yet this is just the tip of the iceberg.

There is confusion and misunderstanding in the media, and amongst politicians and the general public, about what nuclear accidents, particularly the accident at Fukushima, will mean medically. It will be useful to explain how radiation induces disease and what sort of radioactive material is contained in a nuclear power plant.

Fact number one

According to every version of the BIER study by the National Academy of Sciences, up to and including the most recent in 2007 – The Biological Effects of Ionizing Radiation No. V11 (BIER VII) – no dose of radiation is safe. Each dose received by the body is cumulative and adds to the risk of developing malignancy or genetic disease.

Fact number two

Children are ten to twenty times more vulnerable to the carcinogenic effects of radiation than adults. Foetuses are thousands of times more so. Immuno-compromised patients, and the elderly, are also extremely sensitive.

Fact number three

Ionizing radiation from radioactive elements, including radiation emitted from X ray machines and CT scanners, damages living cells. This can result in cancer.

How? Simply speaking, there is a gene in every cell called the regulatory gene. It controls the rate of cell division. If this specific DNA sequence is hit by radiation, the cell will either be killed or, alternatively, the regulatory gene can be bio-chemically altered. This is called a mutation. It is impossible to know if this damage has taken place in your body. The cell will sit silently for many years until, one day, instead of dividing in a controlled fashion, by mitosis, to form two daughter cells, it begins to reproduce uncontrollably, producing trillions of cells. That is a cancer. A single mutation in a single gene can kill you. This process is accelerated in children.

Fact number four
The latent period of carcinogenesis

The incubation time for leukaemia is five to ten years, but for solid cancers (such as breast, lung, thyroid, bone, kidney, and brain) the incubation period ranges from 15 to 70 years. All types of cancer can be induced by radiation.

Fact number five

The reproductive cells in the body, the eggs and sperm, are even more important genetically than normal body cells. Each egg and sperm has only half the number of genes as those in a normal cell so that when they unite, a new normal cell is produced which goes on to form an embryo, then a foetus, then a fully formed baby. Every gene in an egg or sperm cell is precious because these genes control the characteristics of the new individual. Therefore, if normal genes are mutated by radiation the new baby could be born with a genetic disease, or will carry abnormal genes for diseases such as cystic fibrosis and diabetes, or inborn errors of metabolism to be passed on to future offspring. There are over 2,600 genetic diseases now described in the medical literature.

We all carry several hundred genes for genetic disease but, unless we mate with someone carrying the same gene (such as cystic fibrosis), the disease will not become manifest. These abnormal genes have been formed over aeons by background radiation in the environment.

As we increase the level of background radiation in our environment from medical procedures, X-Ray scanning machines at airports, or radioactive materials continually escaping from nuclear reactors and nuclear waste dumps, we will inevitably increase the incidence of cancer as well as the incidence of genetic disease in future generations. Mutated or abnormal genes are passed down from generation to generation in perpetuity.

Fact number six
There are basically five types of ionizing radiation:
1 X-Rays (usually electrically generated), which are non-particulate, and only affect you the instant they pass through your body. You do not become radioactive but your genes may be mutated.
2 Gamma rays, similar to X-Rays, emitted by radioactive materials generated in nuclear reactors and from some naturally occurring radioactive elements in the soil.
3 Alpha radiation, which is particulate, and composed of 2 protons and 2 neutrons, emitted from uranium atoms and from other dangerous elements generated in reactors (such as plutonium, americium, curium, einsteinium, etc – all known as alpha emitters). Alpha particles travel a very short distance in the human body. They cannot even penetrate the layers of dead skin in the epidermis to damage living skin cells. But, if these radioactive elements get into the lung or the liver, bone or other organs, they transfer a large dose of radiation over a long period of time to a very small volume of cells. Most of these cells are killed, but some on the edge of the tiny radiation field will survive. Their genes will be mutated, and cancer may later develop. Alpha emitters are among the most carcinogenic materials known in medicine.
4 Beta radiation, like alpha also particulate, is a charged electron emitted from radioactive elements such as strontium 90, caesium 137, iodine

131, etc. The beta is light in mass, it travels further than an alpha particle but does the same thing, mutates genes.

5 Neutron radiation is released during the fission process in a reactor or a bomb. Reactor 1 at Fukushima is still periodically emitting neutron radiation as sections of the molten core become intermittently critical. Neutrons are large radioactive particles that travel many kilometres, and they pass through everything including concrete, steel etc. There is no way to hide from them and they are extremely mutagenic.

So, let's describe just four of the radioactive elements that are continually being released into the air and water at Fukushima. Remember, though, there are over 100 such elements each with its own characteristics and pathways in the human body. All are invisible, tasteless and odourless.

Caesium 137 is a beta and gamma emitter with a half-life of 30 years. That means in 30 years only half of its radioactive energy has decayed, another 30 years to decay again to half, so it is detectable as a radioactive hazard for some 600 years. For the first 300 years (the standard 10 times the half-life calculation) the levels remain of regulatory concern, but for 300 more years the radiation is still detectable. As there is no safe dose, these levels are still significant and still a hazard. When it lands on the soil it bio-concentrates in grass, fruit and vegetables to many times background levels. It then bio-concentrates tens to thousands of times more, in meat and milk, as animals eat the fruit and vegetation. It concentrates the highest in the human body, the top of the food chain. It is very worrying that it is not, in fact, the adult human body, but that of the newborn infant, which is at the very top of this chain. Because caesium resembles potassium, which is ubiquitous in every cell in our body, it tends to concentrate most highly in brain, muscle, ovary and testicles. There it can cause brain cancer, muscle cancers (rhabdomyosarcomas), ovarian or testicular cancer and, most importantly, mutate genes in the eggs and sperm to cause genetic diseases in future generations.

Strontium 90 is a high-energy beta emitter, half-life 28 years, detectably radioactive for 600 years. As a calcium analogue, it is known as a bone-seeker. It concentrates in the food chain, specifically milk (including breast milk), and is laid down in bones and teeth in the human body, where it can irradiate a bone forming cell, or osteoblast, causing bone cancer; or mutate a white blood cell in the bone marrow which can initiate leukaemia, a cancer of the white blood cells.

Radioactive iodine 131 is a beta and gamma emitter with a half-life of eight days, so it is a hazard for 20 weeks. It bio-concentrates in the food chain, in vegetables and milk, and specifically concentrates in the human thyroid gland where it is a potent carcinogen inducing thyroid disease and thyroid cancer.

Plutonium, one of the most deadly, is an alpha emitter, so toxic that one millionth of a gram will induce cancer if inhaled into the lung. It is transported from the lung by white blood cells, then laid down in thoracic lymph nodes where it can induce Hodgkin's disease or lymphoma. Because it is an iron analogue it combines with the iron transporting protein transferring and concentrates in the liver, a cause of liver cancer; the bone marrow in the haemoglobin molecule, a cause of bone cancer, leukaemia, or multiple myeloma. It concentrates in the testicles and ovaries where it can induce testicular or ovarian cancer, and/or mutate genes to induce genetic disease in future generations. It is one of the few toxic substances that can cross the placental barrier which protects the embryo. Once lodged within the embryo, the alpha particle could kill a cell that would form the left side of the brain, or the right arm – as thalidomide, the morning sickness drug, did years ago.

The half-life of plutonium is 24,400 years, so it can cause harm for 500,000 years; inducing cancers, congenital deformities, and genetic diseases for the rest of time. Not only in humans, but in all life forms.

Plutonium is also fuel for atomic bombs. Five to ten pounds will fuel a weapon which would vaporize a city. Each reactor makes 500 pounds of plutonium a year. It is postulated that one pound of plutonium, if adequately distributed, could kill every person on earth from cancer.

Fact number seven
In summary, the radioactive contamination and fall-out from nuclear power plant accidents will have medical ramifications that will never cease. It will affect future generations, in human terms, forever; inducing epidemics of cancer, leukaemia and genetic disease.

Last thoughts
This is a pivotal time in human history. We watch radiation slowly blanket Japan, a country with four reactors in trouble, in the midst of the worst industrial accident in history, facing an uncertain future of terrible health effects, and catastrophic environmental damage. We watch, helpless, as Fukushima fall-out traverses the Northern Hemisphere, turning up in milk, food, and water; on tourists in airports; and products in shipping bays around the world. We are seeing, and understanding, that all fall-out is local.

There is a reactor in the United States in the middle of the flooding Missouri River, and another just downstream, also in danger should major dams fail. Wildfires recently raged within two miles of the Los Alamos National Laboratory's grounds, a storage place for high and low level nuclear waste from the Cold War, an area where miles and miles of burning land is contaminated by legacy fall-out from atomic testing. Similar wildfires raged over contaminated land in Russia last summer. With ageing nuclear reactors and weapons becoming both more volatile, and more vulnerable, it is time to ask again, this time more forcefully: what is peaceful about nuclear power?

We are staring global warming in the face. Water shortage, famine, rising temperatures, wild weather, and climate refugees in numbers unseen in history are staring back at us. You can't stare down climate change, as the nuclear industry would like to; instead we need to power down our old, wasteful and expensive, dangerous sources of energy and start plugging in to a renewable, sustainable-energy future. We have the money, we have the technology, and we have the time – just barely. If politicians lack the political will, then now is the time for the will of the people to speak louder. There is no other world suitable for life. We either change, or we see the end of this world as we know it.

With grateful acknowledgements to the author for permission to republish. For more discussion of what is happening at Fukushima, and related issues, please see online (www.nuclearfreeplanet.org).

Black Rain

Seiji Takato

The author serves on the Hiroshima Council of A-bomb Sufferers' Organizations. He presented this paper to the World Conference Against Atomic and Hydrogen Bombs in August 2011.

I am now 70 years old, and I was four when I was caught in the radioactive black rain. I lived in a western area of Hiroshima, 8 kilometres from the hypocentre of the nuclear explosion.

That day was very clear. My mother was drying the washing and I was reading a picture book in a room. There was a vivid flash of light. Then sliding paper doors and glass windows fell down on me with a great crash. I hastily went out, crying, to the porch. 'Look at that!' My mother pointed to the sky over the city. We saw yellow light changing into orange, red and light green. It was like an illumination show. In a while, burnt paper, cloth, pieces of wood and ash began to fall. Suddenly, the area around here became dark, and large drops of black rain began to fall. White shirts became black and wet. The water of the river was black and many small fish were floating on their backs with their stomachs turned upwards. This was black rain. It was much later that we discovered the black rain contained radiation.

Because of my poor health, I didn't like going to school in my early elementary school days. Boils formed on my hands and feet. And the lymph glands in my groin and armpits swelled. But I am in good health now.

In Saeki Ward, Hiroshima City, where I live, we formed the Association of Black Rain, with 300 members, eight years ago. At the first meeting survivors talked about how the black rain fell, and the acute disorders they had; high fever, diarrhoea, bloody stools, hair loss. Others talked about the disorders they had later. Many members

◄ *World Conference, Nagasaki, 9 August 2011* (photo: Akiyo Kanamori).

died and now there are less than 250.

Kazuhiro Teramoto, who lives in my neighborhood, was in the third year of elementary school at that time. That morning he saw a strong flash and felt the schoolhouse shake while listening to the teacher. When he came home, in the toilet he wiped his buttocks with the burnt paper that came flying. He ran around a sweet potato field in the rain. The black rain made his shirt very dirty, and he was scolded by his mother because the dirt was difficult to wash out.

Kazuhiro Teramoto felt tired and couldn't wake up in the morning. He was often late for school. He kept coughing, and he couldn't attend gym class in his high school days. Even the doctors of Hiroshima University Hospital couldn't identify the cause of his disease. He was asked, 'Weren't you in Hiroshima City when the A-bomb was dropped? Didn't you go into Hiroshima City soon after the bombing?' He found employment with a major company. But he always felt tired and was labelled a lazy person; he could not help leaving the company. He found work with another company. But the same thing happened to him. His white blood corpuscle count is very high. He suffers from more than ten diseases such as diabetes and liver complaints. He has dialysis treatment daily.

Beneath the mushroom cloud, there was a lot of black rain, radioactive fall-out and minute particles. These were taken into the body through the mouth, respiratory organs, and skin. Low doses of radiation stayed in some parts of the body and were always emitting radiation and damaging the chromosomes. It is called 'internal exposure'. Leukaemia and many other cancers are caused by damaged chromosomes, even decades later.

In 1947, two years after the war ended, the American government established the Atomic Bomb Casualty Commission (ABCC) in Hiroshima and Nagasaki. It was set up purely for scientific research and study; not to provide medical care. They studied many victims who were within 3.5 km from the hypocentre. Based on the research and studies done by the ABCC, the Japanese government said that no after-effects could be found among survivors who were more than 3.5 km from the hypocentre.

A very powerful typhoon hit Hiroshima 42 days after the bombing and washed away surface dirt. Because of this, we insisted that it was impossible to prove that black rain had fallen where we lived. Hiroshima City would not listen to us, and ignored the fact. However, our tenacious movement compelled Hiroshima City to send out questionnaires and interview the survivors. At last, they made a new map with an area six times as large as the original one, and requested that the Japanese government acknowledge the new map. The councils of three cities and four towns where black rain fell did the same thing. The Ministry of Health, Labour and Welfare launched a study group consisting of experts, which has held four meetings.

Kazuhiro Teramoto says,

'When the Fukushima nuclear power plant accident happened, people who live within 30 km from the plant were told to evacuate. But we were not told about the danger of A-bomb radiation. We ate vegetables and drank the water from wells without a lid. Even now I am not recognized as an A-bomb survivor, and I am going to end my hard life. I want my body to be used to study internal exposure, if possible.'

I would like the Japanese government to expand the black rain areas for the survivors in distress, and promote study while survivors are still alive. This is our earnest wish.

The Japanese government should not ignore internal exposure. It will be one of the best ways to promote the research and study of internal exposure, not only for sufferers in Fukushima, but also for Japanese and people all over the world. It will also be a way to abolish nuclear weapons.

A world without nuclear weapons

Hiroshi Taka

On 7 August 2011 in Nagasaki, at a rally to open the second stage of the World Conference against A and H Bombs, thronged with thousands of participants of all ages from all over Japan, the Representative Director of the Japan Council against Atomic and Hydrogen Bombs spoke about the signature campaign in support of the Appeal for a Total Ban on Nuclear Weapons.

Today, conference participants brought with them a large number of signatures in support of a total ban on nuclear weapons, which now are piled up on or in front of this stage. The campaign is continuing in many places at this very moment. The total number of the signatures has exceeded half a million, and reached 548,244 as of 3:30pm this afternoon (7 August 2011). The signatures in boxes piled up in front of you are part of it. On behalf of the people who appended their signatures, I want to convey to you our determination in pursuing the goal of a world without nuclear weapons.

Encouraged by the outcome of the 2010 Non-Proliferation Treaty (NPT) Review Conference in May last year, we started a new signature campaign in support of the 'Appeal for a Total Ban on Nuclear Weapons' on 15 February this year. Blessed by the messages of support from UN Secretary General Ban Ki-moon, UN High Representative Sergio Duarte, Nobel laureates and other distinguished persons in many fields, it was an exciting start. Our motto is 'with the whole of the residents in every region'.

As the World Conference drew near, the campaign quickly gathered momentum: signature drives in the streets on 6th and 9th days in every months were conducted across the country in spite of record-breaking high temperatures; the New Japan Women's Association, which led the last campaign prior to the 2010 NPT Review Conference, has already collected 200,000; the number of the signatures appended by mayors and municipal council leaders has reached 691 and 496 respectively, making a total of 1187.

◄ *On stage at Nagasaki* (photo: Dave Webb)

On the 25th day after the start of the campaign, the huge earthquake and tsunami hit eastern Japan, and the nuclear crisis at the Fukushima Daiichi power plant followed. These incidents became a big challenge even to the campaign. For our movement that was founded to save the *Hibakusha*, it was a task of prime importance to organize support and rescue of the afflicted people. Without wasting time, we took action.

In the meantime, despite spreading fear of radioactivity, A-bomb sufferers in Fukushima were the first who collected signatures and brought them to Fukushima Gensuikyo. People in disaster-afflicted regions in Tohoku and Kanto were undaunted. In spite of the damage from the earthquake, tsunami and the nuclear accident, they continued their annual peace marches, setting out new slogans calling for 'Abolition of Nuclear Weapons', 'Support Rehabilitation from Disaster' and 'Switch to Sustainable Energy'. All these efforts and their messages gave tremendous encouragement to our campaign.

The words of UN Secretary General Ban Ki-moon, at the Riverside Church in New York on 1 May last year, still resound in our ears:

> *'What I see on the horizon is a world free of nuclear weapons.*
> *What I see before me are the people who will help make it happen.*
> *Please keep up your good work.*
> *Sound the alarm, keep up the pressure.*
> *Ask your leaders what they are doing ... personally ... to eliminate the nuclear menace.*
> *Above all, continue to be the voice of conscience.*
> *We will rid the world of nuclear weapons.*
> *And when we do, it will be because of people like you.*
> *The world owes you its gratitude.'*

In September, the 66th session of the UN General Assembly will start. In spring next year, the next round of NPT review process will begin. Making this Conference a new starting point, we will build up a truly community-wide, to a nation-wide campaign, and will bring millions, or even tens of millions of signatures to the UN General Assembly, and to the next NPT Review Conference, as evidence that the people in this, the only A-bombed country, want nuclear weapons to be abolished.

I herewith request warm support and co-operation from you, representatives of the United Nations and national governments, and call on all in this Plenary to renew their determination to generate an explosive development of the campaign.

Appeal for a Total Ban on Nuclear Weapons

In August 1945, two atomic bombs dropped on Hiroshima and Nagasaki instantly turned the two cities into ruins and took the lives of about 210 thousand people. Even now, more than 200,000 Hibakusha, or A-bomb survivors, are carrying with them scars. Their tragedy should not be repeated anywhere on earth.

The call for the elimination of nuclear weapons is becoming ever widespread across the world. Citizens are taking actions, and many governments are endeavouring to reach this goal. The surest guarantee against there being another Hiroshima, or Nagasaki, is a total ban and the elimination of nuclear weapons.

In May 2010, the 189 parties to the Nuclear Non-Proliferation Treaty (NPT), including the Nuclear weapons States, agreed 'to achieve the peace and security of a world without nuclear weapons'. Now is the time to act to accomplish it.

We call on all governments to enter negotiations without delay on a convention banning nuclear weapons.

Please sign at www.antiatom.org

Gensuikyo Signature Campaign

2011 World Conference against A & H Bombs

Declaration of the International Meeting

In the 66th summer since the United States dropped atomic bombs over Hiroshima and Nagasaki, we renew our call on the world to take action to achieve a 'nuclear weapon-free, peaceful and just world'.

The earthquake and tsunami that hit eastern Japan in March took the lives of more than 20,000 people and inflicted catastrophic damage over extensive areas. The highest level nuclear accident at the Fukushima Daiichi nuclear power plant followed it. We offer all the victims our deepest sympathy and condolences. We extend our best wishes and solidarity to the people engaged in post-disaster rehabilitation and reconstruction, and in the effort to bring the nuclear crisis under control and protect the lives of people from radiation exposure.

As the call for a total ban and elimination of nuclear weapons is shared by broader sections of people, including citizens, municipalities and national governments throughout the world, the question of how to achieve a 'nuclear weapon-free world' comes into sharp focus.

The Final Document agreed at the 2010 Non-Proliferation Treaty Review Conference resolved to achieve a 'nuclear weapon-free world,' and called for a special effort to reach that goal. The 65th Session of the UN General Assembly, last year, adopted by an overwhelming majority a resolution calling for a Nuclear Weapons Convention. The Non-Aligned Movement proposes an international conference to discuss ways and means to eliminate nuclear weapons. Many international organizations such as the Mayors for Peace have started serious work on a Nuclear Weapons Convention as an important step towards the abolition of nuclear weapons.

We have been working around the world to urge the nuclear powers and all other governments to start negotiations for a Nuclear Weapons Convention. To date, the signature campaign for the 'Appeal for a Total Ban on Nuclear Weapons' and many varieties of other initiatives are under way, supported by a broad range of people. By further developing these actions in co-operation with the UN and many national governments, let negotiations for the Nuclear Weapons Convention begin immediately and be completed without delay.

Although the agreements reached to date should have been duly implemented, no significant progress has been made. Countries with nuclear weapons are particularly to be held accountable for this stalemate. The repeated sub-critical nuclear tests conducted by the US Obama Administration contradict its own pledge, as well as the spirit of these international agreements.

As long as 'nuclear deterrence' policy persists, 'peace and security in a

◄ *The 'Atomic Dome', Hiroshima* (photo: Dave Webb).

nuclear weapon-free world' cannot be achieved. Instead, it provides incentives to acquire nuclear weapons to counter that policy, and causes nuclear proliferation. The paradox and danger of this policy is clear. We reiterate our demand for a clean break from 'nuclear deterrence' policy by all nations.

While calling for the start of negotiations for a Nuclear Weapons Convention, we demand a ban on the use of nuclear arms, the withdrawal of such weapons deployed on foreign soil, prohibition of the bringing-in and deployment of nuclear weapons in other countries, and the creation of more nuclear-free zones.

We demand the de-alerting of deployed nuclear weapons, further reduction and dismantling of strategic weapons, elimination of tactical nuclear arms, cancellation of modernization and new developments of nuclear weapons, and of the Missile Defence programmes.

The early ratification and entry into force of the Comprehensive Test Ban Treaty, the immediate start of negotiations and conclusion of a fissile material cut-off treaty, and convening of an international conference in 2012 to establish a nuclear weapon-free zone in the Middle East should all be implemented, as agreed upon at the NPT Review Conferences.

The issue of North Korea's nuclear programme should be resolved peacefully through dialogue by restarting the Six-Party Talks.

As the movement that originates from the tragedies of Hiroshima and Nagasaki and calls for the abolition of nuclear weapons, we are deeply concerned about the severity and scope of radioactive contamination and damage caused by the accident at the Fukushima Daiichi nuclear power plant. It has revealed the deceit of the 'safety myth' and the danger of nuclear power plants. It is possible to secure energy sources for sustainable development without recourse to nuclear power and without leaving a dangerous burden to future generations. Let us develop solidarity with the movements in Japan and the rest of the world demanding the decommissioning of nuclear energy and a shift to renewable energy sources.

Japan's peace movement demands that, as the A-bombed country, its government should play due role in concluding a Nuclear Weapons Convention. It also demands the abrogation of secret agreements with the US, which allow nuclear weapons to be brought into Japan, as well as the strict observance of the Three Non-Nuclear Principles. It calls for the dismantling of US military bases in Japan, including the US Marine Corps Futenma Air Station in Okinawa, and opposes the deployment and port-calls of nuclear-powered aircraft carriers and other warships. We express our support for the Japanese peace movement in its efforts for Japan to break away from the US nuclear umbrella and achieve a nuclear-free Japan, and to defend and honour Article 9 of the Constitution of Japan.

Although wars and gunfire continue in different parts of the world, it is no longer time for major powers to prevail in the world by military force.

Opposing the threat or use of force, we demand that conflicts be settled through diplomatic and peaceful means. We support a world order of peace based on the UN Charter, as opposed to military alliances against imaginary enemies.

We extend our warm solidarity to the peoples in North African and Arab countries who stand for freedom, democracy and human dignity. We demand the cessation of NATO's attack on Libya and a ceasefire, and a political solution of the issue.

We oppose the occupation of Iraq and military operations in Afghanistan, and demand the withdrawal of all foreign military forces. Our support goes also to the struggle for the right of the Palestinians to national self-determination, including the right to establish an independent state. We oppose foreign military bases, and stand in solidarity with movements for the defence of national sovereignty and for the removal of such bases. We work in solidarity with movements for relief from war damage, including the victims of Agent Orange.

We call on the people of the world to take the following actions:

– To develop many forms of international, regional and national actions to press for the start of negotiations on a Nuclear Weapons Convention, including the signature campaign for the 'Appeal for a Total Ban on Nuclear Weapons', and to present the achievements of these initiatives to the UN General Assemblies and in the next review process of the Non-Proliferation Treaty.

– To strengthen the movement in each country and region for the removal of nuclear arms and for nuclear-free zones, and develop campaigns and public support for overcoming 'nuclear deterrence' policies.

– To strengthen our activities for the relief, solidarity and support of the *Hibakusha* of Hiroshima and Nagasaki and all nuclear test and radiation victims, to root out any more damage and suffering from radiation. Noting the link between nuclear weapons and nuclear power generation, we oppose military use of nuclear technology and demand an end to the reliance on nuclear energy and a shift to renewable energy sources, and we will work in firm solidarity with a broad range of movements.

The achievement of a 'nuclear weapon-free, peaceful and just world' is the common desire of all who work for peace and against war. It is shared by many people who strive for democracy; human rights; protection of the global environment; women's rights and status; resolution of such issues as hunger, poverty, unemployment, illiteracy and injustice; and for a drastic reduction of military expenditure and armaments and improved social welfare. To achieve this shared goal and to open a new era, let us take bold steps forward, together with the *Hibakusha* and with young people, who bear the future of humanity.

Hiroshima, 5 August 2011

Occupy!

Naomi Klein

Naomi Klein's highy influential book, The Shock Doctrine: The Rise of Disaster Capitalism, *is reviewed, belatedly, by Michael Barratt Brown in this issue. Its relevance is underlined, once again, by the recent destruction in Libya.*

I was honoured to be invited to speak at Occupy Wall Street [in October]. Since amplification is (disgracefully) banned, and everything I said had to be repeated by hundreds of people so others could hear (a.k.a. 'the human microphone'), what I actually said at Liberty Plaza had to be very short. With that in mind, here is the longer, uncut version of the speech.

I love you.

And I didn't just say that so that hundreds of you would shout 'I love you' back, though that is obviously a bonus feature of the human microphone. Say unto others what you would have them say unto you, only way louder.

Yesterday, one of the speakers at the labour rally said: 'We found each other'. That sentiment captures the beauty of what is being created here. A wide-open space (as well as an idea so big it can't be contained by any space) for all the people who want a better world to find each other. We are so grateful.

If there is one thing I know, it is that the 1 per cent loves a crisis. When people are panicked and desperate and no one seems to know what to do, that is the ideal time to push through their wish list of pro-corporate policies: privatizing education and social security, slashing public services, getting rid of the last constraints on corporate power. Amidst the economic crisis, this is happening the world over.

And there is only one thing that can block this tactic, and fortunately, it's a very big thing: the 99 per cent. And that 99 percent is taking to the streets from Madison to Madrid to say 'No. We will not pay for your crisis'.

That slogan began in Italy in 2008. It ricocheted to Greece and France and Ireland and finally it has made its way to the square mile where the crisis began.

'Why are they protesting?' ask the baffled pundits on TV. Meanwhile, the rest of the world asks: 'What took you so long?' 'We've been wondering when you were going to show up.' And most of all: 'Welcome'.

Many people have drawn parallels between Occupy Wall Street and the so-called anti-globalization protests that came to world attention in Seattle in 1999. That was the last time a global, youth-led, decentralized movement took direct aim at corporate power. And I am proud to have been part of what we called 'the movement of movements'. But there are important differences too. For instance, we chose summits as our targets: the World Trade Organization, the International Monetary Fund, the G8. Summits are transient by their nature, they only last a week. That made us transient, too. We'd appear, grab world headlines, then disappear. And in the frenzy of hyper patriotism and militarism that followed the 9/11 attacks, it was easy to sweep us away completely, at least in North America.

Occupy Wall Street, on the other hand, has chosen a fixed target. And you have put no end date on your presence here. This is wise. Only when you stay put can you grow roots. This is crucial. It is a fact of the information age that too many movements spring up like beautiful flowers but quickly die off. It's because they don't have roots. And they don't have long term plans for how they are going to sustain themselves. So when storms come, they get washed away.

Being horizontal and deeply democratic is wonderful. But these principles are compatible with the hard work of building structures and institutions that are sturdy enough to weather the storms ahead. I have great faith that this will happen.

Something else this movement is doing right: you have committed yourselves to non-violence. You have refused to give the media the images of broken windows and street fights it craves so desperately. And that tremendous discipline has meant that, again and again, the story has been the disgraceful and unprovoked police brutality. Which we saw more of just last night. Meanwhile, support for this movement grows and grows. More wisdom.

But the biggest difference a decade makes is that, in 1999, we were taking on capitalism at the peak of a frenzied economic boom. Unemployment was low, stock portfolios were bulging. The media was drunk on easy money. Back then it was all about start-ups, not shut downs.

We pointed out that the deregulation behind the frenzy came at a price. It was damaging to labour standards. It was damaging to environmental standards. Corporations were becoming more powerful than governments and that was damaging to our democracies. But to be honest with you, while the good times rolled, taking on an economic system based on greed was a tough sell, at least in rich countries.

Ten years later, it seems as if there aren't any more rich countries. Just a whole lot of rich people. People who got rich looting the public wealth and exhausting natural resources around the world.

The point is, today, everyone can see that the system is deeply unjust and careening out of control. Unfettered greed has trashed the global economy. And it is trashing the natural world as well. We are overfishing our oceans, polluting our water with fracking and deepwater drilling, turning to the dirtiest forms of energy on the planet, like the Alberta tar sands. And the atmosphere cannot absorb the amount of carbon we are putting into it, creating dangerous warming. The new normal is serial disasters: economic and ecological.

These are the facts on the ground. They are so blatant, so obvious, that it is a lot easier to connect with the public than it was in 1999, and to build the movement quickly.

We all know, or at least sense, that the world is upside down: we act as if there is no end to what is actually finite – fossil fuels and the atmospheric space to absorb their emissions. And we act as if there are strict and immovable limits to what is actually bountiful – the financial resources to build the kind of society we need.

The task of our time is to turn this around: to challenge this false scarcity. To insist that we can afford to build a decent, inclusive society – while at the same time, respect the real limits to what the earth can take.

What climate change means is that we have to do this on a deadline. This time our movement cannot get distracted, divided, burned out or swept away by events. This time we have to succeed. And I'm not talking about regulating the banks and increasing taxes on the rich, though that's important. I am talking about changing the underlying values that govern our society. That is hard to fit into a single media-friendly demand, and it's also hard to figure out how to do it. But it is no less urgent for being difficult.

That is what I see happening in this square. In the way you are feeding each other, keeping each other warm, sharing information freely and providing health care, meditation classes and empowerment training. My favourite sign here says 'I care about you'. In a culture that trains people to avoid each other's gaze, to say, 'Let them die', that is a deeply radical statement.

A few final thoughts. In this great struggle, here are some things that don't matter.

– What we wear.
– Whether we shake our fists or make peace signs.
– Whether we can fit our dreams for a better world into a media soundbite.
   And here are a few things that do matter.
– Our courage.
– Our moral compass.
– How we treat each other.

We have picked a fight with the most powerful economic and political forces on the planet. That's frightening. And as this movement grows from strength to strength, it will get more frightening. Always be aware that there will be a temptation to shift to smaller targets – like, say, the person sitting next to you at this meeting. After all, that is a battle that's easier to win.

Don't give in to the temptation. I'm not saying don't call each other on shit. But this time, let's treat each other as if we plan to work side by side in struggle for many, many years to come. Because the task before will demand nothing less.

Let's treat this beautiful movement as if it is most important thing in the world. Because it is. It really is.

This speech also appeared in Occupied Wall Street Journal *and* The Nation. *It is reprinted here with the author's permission.*

www.naomiklein.org
www.occupywallst.org
www.thenation.com

Academic Freedom?

Noam Chomsky

In April 2011, Professor Chomsky spoke about the implications for academic freedom of the increasing corporatisation of higher education, not least in Britain. These excerpts are taken from his address to the University of Toronto Scarborough in Canada.

A couple of months ago, I went to Mexico to give talks at the National University in Mexico, UNAM. It's quite an impressive university – hundreds of thousands of students, high-quality and engaged students, excellent faculty. It's free. Actually, the government, ten years ago, did try to add a little tuition, but there was a national student strike, and the government backed off. In fact, there's an administrative building on campus that is still occupied by students and used as a centre for activism throughout the city. There's also, in the city itself, another university, which is not only free but has open admissions. It has compensatory options for those who need them. I was there, too; it's also quite an impressive level, students, faculty, and so on. That's Mexico, a poor country.

Right after that I happened to go to California, maybe the richest place in the world. I was giving talks at the universities there. In California, the main universities – Berkeley and University of California, Los Angeles (UCLA) – they're essentially Ivy League private universities; colossal tuition, tens of thousands of dollars, huge endowment. General assumption is they are pretty soon going to be privatized, and the rest of the system will be, which was a very good system – best public system in the world – that's probably going to be reduced to technical training or something like that. The privatization, of course, means privatization for the rich [and a] lower level of mostly technical training for the rest. And that is happening across the country. Next year, for the first time ever, the California system, which was a really great system, best anywhere, is getting more funding from tuition than from the state of California. And that is happening across the country. In most states, tuition covers more than half of the college budget. It's also most of the public research universities. Pretty soon only the community colleges – you know, the lowest level of the system – will be state-financed in any serious sense. And even they're under attack. And analysts generally agree, I'm quoting, 'The era of affordable four-year public universities heavily subsidized by the state may be over'.

Now that's one important way to implement the policy of indoctrination of the young. People who are in a debt trap have very few options. That is true of social control generally; that is also a regular feature of international policy – those of you who study the International Monetary Fund (IMF) and the World Bank and others are well aware. As the Mexico-California example illustrates, the reasons for conscious destruction of the greatest public education system in the world are not economic. Economist Doug Henwood points out that it would be quite easy to make higher education completely free. In the US, it accounts for less than 2 per cent of gross domestic product. The personal share, about 1 per cent of gross domestic product, is a third of the income of the richest 10,000 households. That's the same as three months of Pentagon spending.

It's [also] less than four months of wasted administrative costs of the privatized healthcare system, which is an international scandal. [That system has] about twice the per capita cost of comparable countries, has some of the worst outcomes, and in fact it's the basis for the famous deficit. If the US had the same kind of healthcare system as other industrial countries, not only would there be no deficit, but there would be a surplus. However, to introduce these facts into an electoral campaign would be suicidally insane, Henwood points out. He's correct. In a democracy where elections are essentially bought by concentrations of private capital, it doesn't matter what the public wants. The public has actually been in favour of that for a long of time, but they are irrelevant in a properly run democracy.

We should recall that the great growth period in the economy – the US economy – was in the several decades after World War Two, commonly called the 'Golden Age' by economists. It was substantially fuelled by affordable public education and by university research. Affordable public education includes the GI Bill, which provided free education for veterans – and remember, that was a much poorer country than today. Extremely low tuition fees were found even at private colleges. Actually, I went to an Ivy League college, and it cost $100 a year; that's more now, but it's not that high, it's not 30 or $40,000.

What about university-based research? As I mentioned, that is the core of the modern high-tech economy. That includes computers, the Internet – in fact, the whole IT revolution – and a whole lot more.

The dismantling of this system since the 1970s is among the many moves toward a very sharply two-tiered society, a very narrow concentration of wealth and stagnation for almost everyone else. It also has direct economic consequences. Take, say, California. What they are doing to the public education system is going to undermine the economy that relies on a skilled workforce and creative innovation, Silicon Valley and so on. Apart from the enormous human cost of depriving most people of decent educational opportunities, these policies undermine US competitive capacity. That's very harmful to the mass of the population, but it doesn't matter to the tiny percentage of concentrated wealth and power. In fact, in the years since the Powell Memorandum* [of 1971], we've entered into a new stage in state capitalism in which the future just doesn't amount to much. Profit comes increasingly from financial manipulations. The corporate policies are geared toward short-term profit, and that reduces the concern for loyalty to a firm over a longer stretch. Let me talk about the consequences for education, which are quite significant.

Suppose, as is increasingly happening – not only in the United States, incidentally – that universities are not funded by the state, meaning the general community. So how are the universities going to survive? Universities are parasitic institutions; they don't produce commodities for profit, thankfully. They may one of these days. The funding issue raises many troubling questions, which would not arise if fostering independent thought and inquiry were regarded as a public good, having intrinsic value. That's the traditional ideal of the universities, although there are major efforts to change that. Take Britain. According to the British press, the Arts and Humanities Research Council was just ordered to spend a significant amount of funding on the prime minister's vision for the country. His so-called 'Big Society', which means big corporate profits, and the rest look out for themselves. The government produced what they call a clarification of the famous Haldane Principle. That's the century-old principle that barred such government intrusion into academic research. If this stands, which I think is kind of hard to believe, but if it stands, the hand of Big Brother will rest quite heavily on inquiry and innovation in the arts and humanities as the 'masters of mankind' follow the advice of the Powell Memorandum – of course, defending academic freedom in ways that would receive nods of approval from Those-Who-Must-Not-Be-Named, borrowing my grandchildren's rhetoric. Cameron's Britain is seeking to take the lead on the assault on public education. The rest of the Western world is not very far behind. In some ways the US is ahead.

More generally, in a corporate-run culture, the traditional ideal of free and independent thought may be given lip service, but other values tend to rank higher. Defending authentic institutional freedom is no small task. However, it is not hopeless by any means. I'll talk about the case I know best, at my own university. It is a very striking case, because of the nature of its funding. Technically, it's a private university, but it has vast state funding, overwhelming, particularly since the Second World War. When I joined the faculty over 55 years ago, there were military labs. Since then, they've been technically severed. The academic programs, too, at that time, during the 1950s, were almost entirely funded by the Pentagon. Under student pressure in the 'time of troubles', the 1960s, there were protests about this and calls for investigation. A faculty-student commission was formed in 1969 to investigate the matter. I was a member, thanks in part to student pressure. The commission was interesting. It found that despite the funding source, the Pentagon, almost the entire academic program, there was no military-related work on campus, except in the sense that virtually anything can have some military application. Actually, there was an exception to this. The political science department was deeply engaged in the Vietnam War under the guise of peace research. Since that time, Pentagon funding has been declining, and funding from health-related state institutions – National Institutes of Health and so on – that's been increasing. There's a reason for that. It's reflecting changes in the economy.

In the 1950s and 1960s the cutting edge of the economy was electronics-based. The Pentagon was a natural way to steal money from the taxpayers, making them think they're being protected from the Russians or somebody, and to direct it to eventual corporate profits. That was done very effectively. It includes computers, the Internet, the IT revolution. In fact most of the modern high-tech economy comes from that. In more recent years, the economy is becoming more biology-based. Therefore state funding is shifting. Fifty years ago, if you looked around MIT, you found small electronics start-ups from the faculty. They were drawing on Pentagon funding for research, and if they were successful, they were bought up by major corporations. Those of you who know something about the high-tech economy will know that that's the famous Route 128. That was 50 years ago. Now, if you go around the campus, the start-ups are biology-based, and the same process continues – genetic engineering, biotechnology, pharmaceuticals. The big buildings going up are Novartis and so on. That's the way the so-called free enterprise economy works. There's also been a shift to more short-term applied work. The Pentagon and the National Institutes of Health are concerned with the long-term future of the advanced economy. In contrast, a business firm typically wants something that it can use – it can use and not its competitors, and tomorrow. I don't actually know of a careful study, but it seems pretty clear that the shift towards corporate funding is leading towards more short-term applied research and less exploration of what might turn out to be interesting and important down the road.

Another consequence of corporate funding is more secrecy. This surprises a lot of people, but during the period of Pentagon funding, there was no secrecy. There was also no security on campus. You may remember this. You could walk into the Pentagon-funded labs 24 hours a day, and no cards to stick into things and so on. No secrecy; it was all entirely open. There is secrecy today. A corporation can't compel secrecy, but they can make it very clear that you're not going to get your contract renewed if your work leaks to others. That has happened. In fact, it has led to some scandals, some big enough to appear on the front page of the *Wall Street Journal.*

Outside funding has other effects on the university, unless it's free and unconstrained, observing the Haldane Principle. Indeed, it has been true to a significant degree of funding from the Pentagon and the other national institutions. However, any kind of outside funding [has effects], even keeping to the Haldane Principle. Suppose it establishes a teaching or research facility. That automatically shifts the balance of academic activity, and that can threaten the independence and integrity of the institution. And in the case of corporate funding, quite severely.

Corporatization can have considerable influence in other ways. Corporate managers have a duty. They have to focus on profit-making and seeking to convert as much of life as possible into commodities. It's not because they're bad people; it's their task. Under Anglo-American law, it's their legal obligation as well. There's a lot to say about this topic, but one element of it concerns the universities and much else. One particular consequence is the focus on what's called efficiency. It's an interesting concept. It's not strictly an economic concept. It has crucial ideological dimensions. If a business reduces personnel, it might become more efficient by standard measures with lower costs. Typically, that shifts the burden to the public, a very familiar phenomenon we see all the time. Costs to the public are not counted, and they're colossal. That's a choice that's not based on economic theory. That's based on an ideological decision, which applies directly to the 'business models', as they're called, of the universities. Increasing class-size or employing cheap temporary labour, say graduate students, instead of full-time faculty, may look good on a university budget, but there are significant costs. They're transferred and not measured. They're transferred to students and to the society generally as the quality of education, the quality of instruction, is lowered.

There's, furthermore, no way to measure the human and social costs of converting schools and universities into facilities that produce commodities for the job market, abandoning the traditional ideal of the universities: fostering creative and independent thought and inquiry, challenging perceived beliefs, exploring new horizons and forgetting external constraints. That's an ideal that's no doubt been flawed in practice, but to the extent that it's realized is a good measure of the level of civilization achieved.

That idea is being challenged very openly by Adam Smith's 'principal architects of policy' in the state-corporate complex, the direct attack on the Haldane Principle in Britain. That's an extreme case; in fact so extreme I assume it may be beaten back. There are less blatant examples. Many of them are just inherent in the reliance on outside funding, state or private. These are two sources that are not easy to distinguish given the control of the state by private interest. So what's the right reaction to outside funding that threatens the ideal of a free university? One choice is just to reject it in principle, in which case the university would go down the tubes. It's a parasitic institution. Another choice is just to recognize it as a fact of life that when I'm at work, I have to walk past the Lockheed Martin Lecture Hall, and I have to look out my office window at the Koch building, which is named after the multibillionaires who are the major funders of the Tea Party and a leading force in ongoing campaigns to wipe out the remnants of the labour movement and to institute a kind of corporate tyranny.

Now, if that outside funding seeks to [influence] teaching, research and other activities, then there's a strong argument that it should simply be resisted or rejected outright no matter what the costs. Such influences are not inevitable, and that's worth bearing in mind.

This is a partial transcript. For video of the lecture, go online (www.youtube.com/user/uoftscarborough#p/c/0/Q97tFyqHVLs).

*The confidential Powell Memorandum, entitled 'Attack of American

Free Enterprise System', was composed by Lewis F. Powell, then a corporate lawyer and member of the boards of 11 corporations. It was addressed to Eugene Sydnor, Jr., the Director of the US Chamber of Commerce. The memorandum was dated 23 August 1971, two months prior to Powell's nomination by President Nixon to the US Supreme Court. We reprint a short excerpt below, as this important document may be unfamiliar to readers. The full text is available online: (reclaimdemocracy.org/corporate_accountability/powell_memo_lewis.html).

*   *   *

Attack of Free Enterprise System
Lewis F Powell

Excerpt from the Powell Memo,
also known as the Powell Manifesto, August 1971

The Campus

The assault on the enterprise system was not mounted in a few months. It has gradually evolved over the past two decades, barely perceptible in its origins and benefiting (sic) from a gradualism that provoked little awareness much less any real reaction.

Although origins, sources and causes are complex and interrelated, and obviously difficult to identify without careful qualification, there is reason to believe that the campus is the single most dynamic source. The social science faculties usually include members who are unsympathetic to the enterprise system. They may range from a Herbert Marcuse, Marxist faculty member at the University of California at San Diego, and convinced socialists, to the ambivalent liberal critic who finds more to condemn than to commend. Such faculty members need not be in a majority. They are often personally attractive and magnetic; they are stimulating teachers, and their controversy attracts student following; they are prolific writers and lecturers; they author many of the textbooks, and they exert enormous influence – far out of proportion to their numbers – on their colleagues and in the academic world.

Social science faculties (the political scientist, economist, sociologist and many of the historians) tend to be liberally oriented, even when leftists are not present. This is not a criticism per se, as the need for liberal thought is essential to a balanced viewpoint. The difficulty is that 'balance' is conspicuous by its absence on many campuses, with relatively few members being of conservatives or moderate persuasion and even the relatively few often being less articulate and aggressive than their crusading colleagues.

This situation extending back many years and with the imbalance gradually worsening, has had an enormous impact on millions of young American students. In an article in *Barron's Weekly*, seeking an answer to why so many young people are disaffected even to the point of being revolutionaries, it was said: 'Because they were taught that way'. Or, as noted by columnist Stewart Alsop, writing about his alma mater: 'Yale, like every other major college, is graduating scores' of bright young men ... who despise the American political and economic system'.

As these 'bright young men,' from campuses across the country, seek opportunities to change a system which they have been taught to distrust – if not, indeed 'despise' – they seek employment in the centers of the real power and influence in our country, namely: (i) with the news media, especially television; (ii) in government, as 'staffers' and consultants at various levels; (iii) in elective politics; (iv) as lecturers and writers, and (v) on the faculties at various levels of education.

Many do enter the enterprise system – in business and the professions – and for the most part they quickly discover the fallacies of what they have been taught. But those who eschew the mainstream of the system often remain in key positions of influence where they mold public opinion and often shape governmental action. In many instances, these 'intellectuals' end up in regulatory agencies or governmental departments with large authority over the business system they do not believe in.

If the foregoing analysis is approximately sound, a priority task of business – and organizations such as the Chamber – is to address the campus origin of this hostility. Few things are more sanctified in American life than academic freedom. It would be fatal to attack this as a principle. But if academic freedom is to retain the qualities of 'openness,' 'fairness' and 'balance' – which are essential to its intellectual significance – there is a great opportunity for constructive action. The thrust of such action must be to restore the qualities just mentioned to the academic communities.

Apartheid in South Africa and Palestine?

John Dugard

*John Dugard is a South
African international
lawyer who headed the
Centre for Applied Legal
Studies in Johannesburg
during the Apartheid era.
In 1995 he assisted in the
drafting of the Bill of
Rights in the South
African Constitution. For
seven years he was
Special Rapporteur on the
human rights situation in
the Occupied Palestinian
Territory to the UN
Human Rights Council
and Commission on
Human Rights.
Professor Dugard gave
evidence to the Third
Session of the Russell
Tribunal on Palestine,
which met in Cape Town
from 5 to 7 November
2011. The theme of the
Session was Israel and
Apartheid under
international law.*

I spent most of my adult life in South Africa opposing apartheid, as an advocate, legal academic and, from 1978-1990, director of the Centre for Applied Legal Studies (a research institute engaged in human rights advocacy and litigation). In my work I compared and contrasted apartheid with international human rights standards and advocated a Constitution with a Bill of Rights in a democratic South Africa. Unlike many other South Africans, I was never imprisoned but I was prosecuted, arrested and threatened by the security police. My major book, *Human Rights and the South African Legal Order* (1978), the most comprehensive account of the law and practice of apartheid, was initially banned.

I had wide experience and knowledge of the three pillars of the apartheid state – racial discrimination, repression and territorial fragmentation. I led lawyers' campaigns against the eviction of black persons from neighbourhoods set aside for exclusive white occupation by the Group Areas Act, and against the notorious 'pass laws', which made it an offence for blacks to be in so-called 'white areas' without the correct documentation. These campaigns took the form of free legal defence to all those arrested, which made the systems unmanageable. Through the Centre for Applied Legal Studies I engaged in legal challenges to the implementation of the security laws and emergency laws, which allowed detention without trial and house arrest – and, in practice, torture. I also challenged the establishment of Bantustans in the courts.

After South Africa became a democracy, I was appointed to a small committee of experts charged with the task of drafting a Bill of Rights for the 1996 South African Constitution.

I visited Israel and the Occupied Palestinian Territory in 1982, 1984, 1988 and 1998 to participate in conferences on issues affecting the region In 2001, I was appointed as Chair of a Commission of Enquiry established by the Commission on Human Rights to investigate human rights violations during the Second Intifada. I was also appointed as Special Rapporteur to the Commission on Human Rights (later Human Rights Council) on the human rights situation in the Occupied Palestinian Territory. In this capacity I visited the Occupied Palestinian Territory twice a year and reported to the Commission and the Third Committee of the General Assembly. My mandate expired in 2008. In February 2009, I lead a Fact-Finding Mission established by the League of Arab States to investigate and report on violations of human rights and humanitarian law in the course of Operation Cast Lead.

From my first visit to Israel/the Occupied Palestinian Territory I was struck by the similarities between apartheid in South Africa and the practices and policies of Israel in the Occupied Palestinian Territory. These similarities became more obvious as I became better informed about the situation. As Special Rapporteur I deliberately refrained from making such comparisons until 2005, as I feared that such comparisons would prevent many governments in the West from taking my reports seriously. However, after 2005 I decided that I could not, in good conscience, refrain from making such comparisons.

Of course, the two regimes are very different. Apartheid South Africa was a state that practised discrimination and repression against its own people. Israel is an occupying power that controls a foreign territory and its people under a regime recognized by international humanitarian law. But in practice there is little difference. Both regimes were/are characterized by discrimination, repression and territorial fragmentation. The main difference is that the apartheid regime was more honest. The law of apartheid was openly legislated in Parliament and was clear for all to see, whereas the law governing Palestinians in the Occupied Palestinian Territory is largely contained in obscure military decrees and inherited emergency regulations that are virtually inaccessible.

In my work as Commissioner and Special Rapporteur I saw every aspect of the occupation of the Occupied Palestinian Territory. I witnessed the humiliating checkpoints, which reminded me of the implementation of the pass laws (but worse), separate roads (unknown in apartheid South Africa), and the administrative demolition of houses, which reminded me of the demolition of houses in 'black areas' set aside for exclusive white occupation. I visited Jenin in 2003 shortly after it had been devastated by the Israeli Defence Force. I spoke to families whose houses had been raided, and vandalized by the IDF; I spoke to young and old who had been tortured by the IDF; and I visited hospitals to see those who had been wounded by the IDF. I saw and, on occasion, visited settlements; I saw most of the Wall and spoke to farmers whose lands had been seized for the construction of the Wall; and I travelled through the Jordan Valley viewing destroyed Bedouin camps and checkpoints designed to serve the interests of the settlers.

A final comment based on my personal experience. There was an altruistic element to the apartheid regime, albeit motivated by the ideology of separate development, which aimed to make the Bantustans viable states. Although not in law obliged to do so, it built schools, hospitals and roads for black South Africans. It established industries in the Bantustans to provide employment for blacks. Israel even fails to do this for Palestinians. Although in law it is obliged to cater for the material needs of the occupied people, it leaves this all to foreign donors and international agencies. Israel practises the worst kind of colonialism in the Occupied Palestinian Territory. Land and water are exploited by an aggressive settler community that has no interest in the welfare of the Palestinian people – with the blessing of the state of Israel.

Copyright John Dugard, with grateful acknowledgements

This article originally appeared in Al-Majdal, a magazine concerned with Palestinian residency and refugee rights.

www.badil.org/al-majdal/
www.russelltribunalonpalestine.com

The 'great game' in Syria

Alastair Crooke

Alastair Crooke is founder and director of Conflicts Forum, and the author of Resistance: The Essence of the Islamist Revolution *(Pluto Press). He worked for the British Secret Intelligence Service (MI6), and was later an adviser to the European Union's Foreign Policy Chief, Javier Solana, from 1997 to 2003.*

This summer, a senior Saudi official told John Hannah[1], former United States vice president Dick Cheney's former chief-of-staff, that from the outset of the Syrian upheaval in March, the king has believed that regime change in Syria would be highly beneficial to Saudi interests: 'The king knows that other than the collapse of the Islamic Republic itself, nothing would weaken Iran more than losing Syria,' said the official.

This is today's 'great game': the formula for playing it has changed; the US-instigated 'colour' revolutions in the former Soviet republics have given way to a bloodier, and more multi-layered process today, but the underlying psychology remains unchanged.

The huge technical requirements of mounting such a complex game in Syria are indeed prodigious: but in focusing so closely on technique and on co-ordinating diverse interests, inevitably something important may recede from view, too.

Europeans and Americans and certain Gulf states may see the Syria game as the logical successor to the supposedly successful Libya 'game' in remaking the Middle East, but the very tools that are being used on their behalf are highly combustible and may yet return to haunt them – as was experienced in the wake of the 1980s 'victory' in Afghanistan.

It will not be for the first time that Western interests sought to use others for their ends, only to find they have instead been used.

In any event, the tactics in Syria, in spite of heavy investment, seem to be failing. Yet Western strategy, in response to the continuing cascade of new events in the region, remains curiously static, grounded in gaming the awakening and tied ultimately to the fragile thread connecting an 88-year-old king to life.

There seems to be little thought about the strategic landscape when, and as, that thread snaps. We may yet see the prevailing calculus turned inside out: nobody knows. But does the West really believe that being tied into a model of Gulf monarchical legitimacy and conservatism in an era of popular disaffection to be a viable posture – even if those states do buy more Western weapons?

What then is the new anatomy of the great game? In the past, colour revolutions were largely blueprinted in the offices of the political consultancies of 'K' Street in Washington. But in the new format, the 'technicians' attempting to shape the region[2] hail directly from the US government: according to reports by senior official sources in the region, Jeffrey Feltman, a former ambassador in Lebanon, and presently assistant secretary of state, as chief co-ordinator[3], together with two former US ambassadors, Ron Schlicher and David Hale, who is also the new US Middle East Peace Envoy.

And instead of an operations centre established in some phony 'Friends of Syria' organization established in Washington, there is a gold-plated operations centre located in Doha, financed, according to a number of sources, by big Qatari money.

The origins of the present attempt to refashion the Middle East lie with the aftermath of Israel's failure in 2006 to seriously damage Hezbollah. In the post-conflict autopsy, Syria was spotlighted as the vulnerable lynchpin connecting Hezbollah to Iran. And it was Prince Bandar of Saudi Arabia who planted the first seed: hinting to US officials that something indeed might be done about this Syria connector, but only through using the Syrian Muslim Brotherhood, adding quickly in response to the predictable demurs, that managing the Syrian Brotherhood and other Islamists could safely be left to him.

John Hannah noted on ForeignPolicy.com[4] that 'Bandar working without reference to US interests is clearly cause for concern; but Bandar working as a partner against a common Iranian enemy is a major strategic asset'. Bandar was co-opted.

Hypothetical planning suddenly metamorphosed into concrete action only earlier this year, after the fall of Saad Hariri's government in Lebanon, and the overthrow of president Hosni Mubarak in Egypt: suddenly, Israel seemed vulnerable, and a weakened Syria, enmired in troubles, held a strategic allure.

In parallel, Qatar had stepped to the fore, as Azmi Bishara, a pan-Arabist, former Israeli parliament member, expelled from the Knesset and now established in Doha, architected a schema through which television – as various in the Arabic press have reported[5] – that is, al-Jazeera, would not just report revolution, but instantiate it for the region – or at least this is what was believed in Doha in the wake of the Tunisia and Egyptian uprisings.

This was a new evolution over the old model: hubristic television, rather than mere media management. But Qatar was not merely trying to leverage human suffering into an international intervention by endlessly repeating 'reforms are not enough' and the 'inevitability' of Assad's fall, but also – as in Libya – Qatar was directly involved as a key operational actor and financier.

The next stage was to draw French President Nikolas Sarkozy into the campaign through the emir of Qatar's expansive nature and ties to Sarkozy, supplemented by Feltman's lobbying. An 'Elysée team' of Jean-David Levite, Nicholas Gallet and Sarkozy, was established, with Sarkozy's wife enlisting Bernard Henri-Levy, the arch promoter of the Benghazi Transitional Council model that had been so effective in inflating the North Atlantic Treaty Organization (NATO) into an instrument of regime change.

Finally, President Barack Obama delegated Turkey[6] to play point on Syria's border. Both of the latter components, however, are not without their challenges from their own security arms, who are sceptical of the efficacy of the Transitional Council model, and opposed to military intervention.

The Turkish leadership, in particular, is pushed by party pressures in one direction[7], whilst at another there are deep misgivings about Turkey becoming a NATO 'corridor' into Syria. Even Bandar is not without challenges: he has no political umbrella from the king, and others in the family are playing other Islamist cards to different ends.

In operational terms, Feltman and his team co-ordinate, Qatar hosts the 'war room', the 'news room' and holds the purse strings, Paris and Doha lead on pushing the Transitional Council model, whilst Bandar[8] and Turkey jointly manage the Sunni theatre in-country, both armed and unarmed.

The Salafist component of armed and combat experienced fighters was to have been managed within this framework, but increasingly they went their own way, answering to a different agenda, and having separate finances.

If the scope of the Syria 'game' – for let us not forget the many killed (including civilians, security forces, and armed fighters) make it no game – is on a different scale to the early 'colour' revolutions, so its defects are greater too. The National Transitional Council paradigm, already displaying its flaws in Libya, is even more starkly defective in Syria, with the opposition 'council' put together by Turkey, France and Qatar caught in a catch-22 situation. The Syrian security structures have remained rock solid[9] through seven months – defections have been negligible – and Assad's popular support base is intact.

Only external intervention could change that equation, but for the opposition to call for it would be tantamount to political suicide, and they know it. Doha and Paris[10] may continue to try to harass the world towards some intervention by maintaining attrition but the signs are that the internal opposition will opt to negotiate.

But the real danger in all this, as John Hannah himself notes on ForeignPolicy.com[11], is that the Saudis, 'with their back to the wall', 'might once again fire up the old jihadist network and point it in the general direction of Shi'ite Iran'.

In fact, that is exactly what is happening, but the West does not seem to have noticed. As *Foreign Affairs* noted recently, Saudi and its Gulf allies are 'firing up' the Salafists[12], not only to weaken Iran, but mainly in order to do what they see is necessary to survive – to disrupt and emasculate the awakenings which threaten absolute monarchism.

Salafists are being used for this end in Syria[13], in Libya, in Egypt (see their huge Saudi flag waving turn-out in Tahrir Square in July)[14] in Lebanon, Yemen[15] and Iraq.

Salafists may be generally viewed as non-political and pliable, but history is far from comforting. If you tell people often enough that they shall be the king-makers in the region and pour buckets-full of money at them, do not be surprised if they then metamorphose – yet again – into something very political and radical.

Michael Scheuer, the former head of the Central Intelligence Agency Bin Laden Unit, recently warned[16] that the Hillary Clinton-devised response to the Arab awakening, of implanting Western paradigms, by force if necessary, into the void of fallen regimes, will be seen as a 'cultural war on Islam' and will set the seeds of a further round of radicalization.

Saudi Arabia is America's ally. The US, as friends, should ask them if the fall of Assad, and the sectarian conflict that is almost certain to ensue, is really in their interest: do they imagine that their Sunni allies in Iraq and

Lebanon will escape the consequences? Do they really imagine that the Shi'ites of Iraq will not put two-and-two together and take harsh precautions?

One of the sad paradoxes to the sectarian 'voice' adopted by the Gulf leaders to justify their repression of the awakening has been the undercutting of moderate Sunnis, now caught between the rock of being seen as a Western tool, and the hard place of Sunni Salafists just waiting for the chance to displace them.

This article was first posted on Asia Times Online, 22 October 2011. It is reprinted with the author's permission.

www.conflictsforum.org

Notes
1 See shadow.foreignpolicy.com
2 See thecable.foreignpolicy.com
3 See www.champress.net and www.haaretz.com
4 See shadow.foreignpolicy.com
5 Qataris seeking alternative for Waddah Khanfar to manage Al-Jazeera, Al-Intiqad, 20 September 2011.
6 See www.foreignaffairs.com
7 See en.rian.ru
8 See shadow.foreignpolicy.com
9 See www.joshualandis.com
10 See euobserver.com
11 See shadow.foreignpolicy.com
12 See www.foreignaffairs.com
13 See euobserver.com
14 See www.washingtonpost.com
15 See www.foreignaffairs.com
16 See nationalinterest.org

Iraq's Report X

Brian Jones

Dr Jones was head of the UK Defence Intelligence Staff's nuclear, biological and chemical weapons section in the build up to the invasion and occupation of Iraq. Since 2003, he has maintained a constant flow of objective comment on the use and misuse of intelligence during that period. For anyone seeking a reliable guide through this labyrinth, his book, Failing Intelligence, *is the best place to start.*

Evidence released earlier this year by Sir John Chilcot's Iraq Inquiry reinforces the suspicion I first raised publicly in 2004 that Defence Intelligence Staff (DIS) analysts, and probably some members of the Joint Intelligence Committee (JIC) (and hence the wider audience – cabinet, parliament, public) were deceived into believing that the evidence of Saddam's possession of weapons of mass destruction (WMD) was stronger than it actually was.

To recap: throughout the drafting of the September 2002 dossier, DIS analysts argued that the assessment of Iraq's WMD status and capability was being expressed in terms that were not warranted by the available intelligence. The DIS representatives at the final drafting meeting refused to endorse the assessment and clear the dossier. In an attempt to persuade them, they were told a recently received intelligence report from MI6, which could not be released to them, overcame their reservations about whether Iraq actually possessed any chemical and biological weapons. (For convenience, I have previously referred to this intelligence as Report X and will continue to do so here). They rightly said they could not change the DIS position under such circumstances. As a result, after the meeting a representative of MI6, which had been at the drafting meeting, spoke with a senior manager in the DIS about the new intelligence and this led to the Chief of Defence Intelligence, on the advice of his Deputy, approving the draft of the dossier without further reference to his analysts.

The 2004 Butler Review said it was presented with no 'evidence that persuaded the committee that there was an insuperable obstacle to allowing analysts access to the intelligence' (page 139, para 577) and 'it was wrong that a report which was of significance in the drafting of a document of the importance of the dossier was not shown to key experts in the DIS who could have commented on the validity and credibility of the report' (page 111, para 452). The decision meant it 'was not seen by the few people in the UK intelligence community able to form an all-round, professional technical judgement on its reliability and significance' (page 138, para 575). Butler also noted that it was known at the outset that the intelligence on which Report X was based came from a source without a proven record of reliability. Sir Richard Dearlove, the Head of MI6 at the time, has insisted that he made this clear to those he spoke to about it, including Prime Minister Blair, his foreign policy adviser, Sir David Manning, his chief of staff Jonathan Powell, his head of communications Alastair Campbell and John Scarlett, Chairman of the JIC. In other words, Butler believed those who did see Report X were not properly qualified to analyse it and those who decided that it was necessary to exclude the expert analysts made an error of judgement.

Butler revealed that Report X indicated 'the production of biological and chemical agent had been accelerated by the Iraqi Government, including through the building of further facilities throughout Iraq' (page138, para 573). Despite the fact that it was later withdrawn and discredited, the content of Report X remains a matter of the highest importance. The Butler review said Report X had provided 'significant assurance to those drafting the Government's dossier that active, current production of chemical and biological agent was taking place' (page 100, para 405) and 'The fact that it was not shown to … [Brian Jones and colleagues] resulted in a stronger assessment in the dossier in relation to Iraqi chemical weapons production than was justified by the available intelligence' (page 139, para 577). The implication is that those concerned recognised that the WMD assessment was unsustainable without the degree of certainty added by Report X if it proved to be right. This means it was a key element in the dossier, which would become the most comprehensive written declaration of the government's case for war.

Unfortunately, for reasons that require explanation, Butler avoided offering an opinion on whether those who had seen Report X were justified in believing it to be valid and credible and justified overruling the assessment of the DIS expert analysts and modifying the previous JIC position. Despite calls in the House of Commons in 2004 for the report to be released, it never has been. Seven years on, the transcripts of the private interviews are taking us beyond what was revealed by Butler. They suggest that Report X fell well short of providing the convincing evidence about Iraq's WMD which would have been necessary to dismiss the analysts' concerns. What they have said reinforces the suspicion I had at the time that an inconclusive intelligence report was being used incompetently or dishonestly to finesse the DIS objections.

The most important information comes from private interviews with a number of senior members of the MI6 (Secret Intelligence Service) who were involved in 2001-3 and are identified by the assignment of SIS numbers rather than names, and with their boss, Sir Richard Dearlove. Some revelations were also made by the Inquiry committee during the course of their questioning. Despite being heavily redacted, the transcripts are none the less revealing .

Dearlove believed that the intelligence in Report X placed them 'on the edge of a significant breakthrough' (see SIS4 transcript 1, page 56). Several of his officers appeared to suggest the intelligence was non-specific and believed when the dossier was published a breakthrough was still needed on, for example, the location of agent production facilities. It was hoped the new source would provide more specific information which would allow analysts to cross-check the data and reach a more confident and convincing assessment that Iraq possessed chemical and biological weapons. It was described by SIS1 (p18) as 'wishful thinking' that the source would come good on his promise to provide the 'crock of gold at the end of the rainbow'. However, none of the MI6 witnesses, or those questioning them, directly linked Report X to the dossier that was being produced at this time (unless that was buried in the redactions).

Report X was issued on 11 September 2002 and, at the suggestion of Manning, it was briefed by Dearlove to the Prime Minister during a meeting on 12 September. Blair has never acknowledged the significance of Report X. When asked by the Iraq Inquiry about the 12 September meeting, he spoke of the impact on him of new intelligence of mobile production facilities for biological weapons rather than recalling anything about the sensitive source of Report X. However, during questioning of two other MI6 witnesses, a member of the Inquiry appeared to suggest to one of them that it had evidence that both the Prime Minister and Foreign Secretary displayed particular interest in this intelligence, especially whether the promised 'silver bullet' had materialised or when it might be expected (see SIS 4 transcript 1, page 58). SIS1 (page 60) revealed that the Prime Minister had mentioned it to him as late as January 2003. At the Hutton Inquiry, Alastair Campbell's recollection of the 12 September meeting gave prominence to the Report X intelligence and attributed to Dearlove the notion that it could not be used in the dossier directly but might be used 'through assertion'. Campbell said Dearlove told them this was because of the sensitivity of the source, however, there must now be suspicion that the real reason was because of the uncertain nature of the information. Whichever it was, the absence of information that eliminated doubt, and the requirement for the 'silver bullet' remains evident. It is to be hoped the Inquiry will clarify what was discussed at that 12 September 2002 meeting and its importance to the stated confidence in the assessed status of Iraq's WMD capability that appeared in the dossier (including its Foreword).

When the source was seen again and a second report issued towards the end of September (Report Y, perhaps) the information fell far short of being the 'silver bullet' needed. This may have been what led to the change from the unqualified judgement in the dossier of 24 September that 'Iraq has continued to produce chemical and biological agents', to a JIC assessment on 28 October which said 'intelligence *indicates* that [Iraq] has continued to produce chemical agent' (Butler page 88, paragraph 346) and 'intelligence *indicates* it has continued to produce biological agents' (Butler page 88, paragraph 348) [my italics]. For an experienced JIC reader, the use of the word 'indicates' weakens the judgement considerably. Report Y must have remained firmly in its compartment of limited readership during the period at least up to my retirement in January 2003 and, I suspect, until after the war. No explanation for the modification of the assessment between 24 September and 28 October was volunteered at the time to DIS analysts by CDI or his Deputy. For my part, in October/November 2002 I recall that I was pleased that a normal JIC assessment had more closely reflected our analysis.

Beyond the protection of the incompetent or the guilty, there can be few reasons now why suitably redacted versions of Reports X, Y, and a report ('Z'), which apparently summarised them and was given a wider distribution in about April 2003, cannot be made available for public scrutiny. The critical information they contain has become historic. Its source appears to have misled us into a damaging war with many deaths and can deserve little further consideration or protection. Any remaining risk should be balanced against the need to resolve a matter that continues to undermine the confidence of the British public in intelligence, politicians and officials. If the Inquiry cannot disclose a redacted but substantial version of the reports, it should make much clearer and complete statements on this issue than its predecessors have. And parliament must satisfy itself that the national interest has been served by what has been revealed.

The failure of four inquiries to deal with this issue suggests that those concerned who saw Report X or were briefed about it in September 2002 have repeatedly failed to reveal important information over many inquiries and years. The previous inquiries have either failed to uncover the full truth or decided not to reveal it to Parliament or the public at large. It is important that the current inquiry examines and explains why these details have not emerged in a more timely fashion.

Whilst the detail relating to the intelligence is mainly about the behaviour of officials, what happened does raise the question of the diligence of Blair and other ministers in reading intelligence reports, JIC assessments and the draft dossier with an appropriately critical eye. The information contained in them did not indicate certainty about Iraq's WMD. If Blair gained his confidence by attaching greater weight to verbal briefings by individuals and small groups rather than carefully prepared documentary briefs and reports then Chilcot should make that clear. The Inquiry should make explicit judgements on whether ministerial and/or civil service codes of conduct have been breached.

Editor's note: The Chilcot Inquiry seems to have entered a long hibernation. Nothing has appeared on its website since July 2011, and newspaper stories suggest its report might be delayed until summer 2012. By contrast, Iraqi Inquiry Digest maintains a steady flow of informative and probing commentary online, including from Dr Jones.

* * *

Michael D. Higgins
President of Ireland

Roger Cole, Chair of Ireland's Peace and Neutrality Alliance (PANA) said:

'PANA welcomes the election of Michael D. Higgins as President of Ireland. Michael D. Higgins consistently opposed the use of Shannon Airport by US troops in the wars in Afghanistan and Iraq, and has called for the withdrawal of Irish troops from Afghanistan. These have been key demands of the Irish peace movement since 2001. The Irish Constitution commits us to the peaceful resolution of international disputes and we would hope that his election symbolises the restoration of the values of Irish Independence, democracy and neutrality, and the rejection of the neo-liberal militarist ideology that has dominated our political élite for so long.'

www.pana.ie

Building Bridges

Stephanie Sampson

The author is an independent researcher and writer.

What was The Atlantic Bridge? How did this bogus 'charity' operate without question for years? And who were the donors?

During recent times, we have learnt that the former Secretary of State for Defence, Liam Fox, resigned from his position after accusations that he had breached the Ministerial Code by allowing his close friend, (lobbyist and businessman) Adam Werritty, to represent himself as Fox's adviser and accompany him to official defence meetings (including to Dubai, Israel and Washington[1]) despite not being employed in any official capacity. An official report by Gus O'Donnell found that Fox indeed breached these rules by failing to ensure that no conflict of interest arose.[2] Apologies have been made and Liam Fox has accepted personal responsibility and the conclusions of the Cabinet Secretary's Report.[3]

O'Donnell's Report, however, is seen to be superficial for not addressing the issues and questions that are on everyone's mind. Namely, what exactly was The Atlantic Bridge? Who were the donors? And did anyone profit from Fox's decisions as Defence Minister?

What was The Atlantic Bridge? Founded in 1997 by Fox, the 'Atlantic Bridge Research and Education Scheme' was a 'think-tank', with Margaret Thatcher as Honorary Patron. The organisation proclaimed to espouse the 'Special Relationship' between the United States and the United Kingdom – a phrase coined by Winston Churchill in 1945 and used in his 1946 speech, which focused particularly on aiding the United States to guard the atomic bomb *'as a sacred trust for the maintenance of peace'* and the *'continuance of the intimate relationship between our military advisers, leading to common study of potential dangers [and] the similarity of weapons and manuals of instructions'.*[4] In recent years, this 'Special Relationship' has come to exemplify the Thatcher-Reagan partnership that flourished in the 1980s – namely the promotion of neoliberal projects including privatisation, reduced state intervention, advancing the 'free market', and a shared hostility towards communism.

The Atlantic Bridge (TAB) gained charity status on 3 February 2003, and sought the *'furtherance of public education on both sides of the Atlantic, in areas of common interest, focusing particularly but not exclusively on free trade, economics, health and science'*, with emphasis on public education and research.[5] Following a complaint in August 2009 to the Charity Commission (the 'Commission') by online blogger Stephen Newton[6] (who took note of TAB's affiliations, dubbing it the 'Tory Travel Club'), an investigation ensued, and the Commission published its findings on 26 July 2010. Political purposes can never be charitable, and if TAB were truly a charitable organisation, it would had to have demonstrated that it was not political in nature; that it operated for the public benefit to further charitable purposes; and that it disseminated information gathered from events and lectures available to the public. All evidence pointed contrary to this – with the Commission's Report looking particularly at an article published in *The Washington Examiner* by the Chief Executive of the US arm of TAB, Amanda Bowman. The article was political in nature, published just before the UK General Election in May 2010; she discussed the benefits to the US of a British Conservative government, stating that *'Cameron will be much more amenable to shared US-UK foreign interests than [Gordon] Brown'.*[7]

Furthermore, the information on TAB's website was scarce, not readily available to the general public, and the messages conveyed in TAB's lectures by politicians were not considered to be neutral and balanced in manner, as they promoted a particular (right-wing, Atlanticist) point of view.[8] It was for these reasons that the Commission advised TAB's activities 'cease immediately'.

It can safely be said that this was a case of political propaganda, masquerading as education, in order to achieve a privileged charity status. It is hard to understand how this 'charity' went unquestioned for so long when its political agenda was so explicit; particularly when organisations meeting the 'charity criteria', who campaign for improvement in public policy, are denied charity status on the grounds that such a trust could jeopardise relations with another country.[9]

The Bridge

The Atlantic Bridge website boasted a *'network of like-minded people in politics, business, academia and journalism who come together to share views and experiences ... in order to promote an agenda that will strengthen the Special Relationship'*, drawing on the *'expertise'* of their membership.[10] From the start, this 'Special Relationship' has clearly been promoted through neo-conservative, right-wing ideology, with a political agenda, run by high-profile politicians and businessmen. All parties involved over the years could have benefited from this 'Special Relationship', as politicians and lobbyists (the 'like-minded people') at the forefront of the organisation have attended numerous ceremonies and meetings in the name of 'championing freedom in a rapidly changing world'.

There are many UK Conservatives who have played a part within TAB, including Cabinet Ministers Michael Gove, Chris Grayling, William Hague and George Osborne, Second Defence Minister Lord Astor, as well as Andrew Dunlop (former Thatcher adviser and lobbyist). Notable US Republican participants included Senator Jon Kyl (the 'great persuader', recognised as one of the most influential people in the world by *Time Magazine* for his persuasive role in the Senate[11]); Senator Joe Lieberman (a 'powerful proponent for robust Pentagon spending and weapons programs', 'friend of defence contractors' and recipient of $250,000 in donations from military contractor United Technologies[12]) and John Falk (defence lobbyist and managing director of private security and defence firm Kestral) to name a few. In line with TAB's mission statement, it can be seen that each of these individuals had their own areas of *'expertise'*, and were there to *'promote an agenda that would strengthen the Special Relationship'*.

Not only was TAB politically biased in its membership, the charity also handed out Margaret Thatcher 'Medals of Freedom' at ceremonies in London to notable right-wing figures, including Henry Kissinger and Rudy Giuliani. Kissinger received his award in 2009 for his *'tireless dedication to academia, public service and peace'*. While Giuliani, at his reception, said that he would like to increase the size of the US military.[13]

It was not just award ceremonies that offered a good chance for Tories and lobbyists to meet and greet their American counterparts – events and conferences attracted sponsorship from Lehman Brothers and the Heritage Foundation; speakers from the Center for Security Policy; donations from

US multinational pharmaceutical corporation Pfizer, from hedge fund boss Michael Hintze (represented by Lord Bell, former Thatcher adviser and head of public relations firm, Bell Pottinger), and from a one-time vice chairman of the lobby group Britain Israel Communications and Research Centre (Bicom), Michael Lewis (also a significant donor to the Conservative party).[14]

The charity's history is littered with donations from companies who share a *'common interest'* with TAB's members and associates. In 2010, Liam Fox accepted a £50,000 donation from venture capitalist Jon Moulton, whose firm Better Capital now owns an aerospace, military manufacturer, Gardner Aerospace.[15]

In 2007, after Werritty was appointed as UK Executive Director of The Atlantic Bridge, donations rose from £3,309 in 2006 to £49,666 in 2007[16]; interestingly, it was also in 2007 that TAB formed an alliance with powerful lobbying organisation the American Legislative Exchange Council (ALEC) and formed a sister charity, 'Atlantic Bridge Inc'. It was after the formation of this partnership that true intentions became clearer; ALEC's maxim is 'limited government, free markets, federalism'; its funders include Exxon Mobil, Phillip Morris tobacco and the National Rifle Association. ALEC was found to have held conventions in order to mingle with legislators, presenting them with pre-drafted bills on behalf of members – out of 1000 bills, it is reckoned that some 20% became law.[17]

The US's Atlantic Bridge Inc. closed down in December 2010, and in the UK The Atlantic Bridge was dissolved on 30 September 2011, just over 12 months since the publication of the Charity Commission's initial findings. It looks likely that its last months were spent tying up loose ends, with associated UK Conservatives seemingly anxious to distance themselves from the organisation. The Commission's report failed to expose the real issues and, after the dissolution, failed to address which charity TAB's remaining assets (£36,000[18]) were transferred to. It could just be coincidence that Pargav, an organisation established by Werritty to further Fox's interest in foreign policy whilst guaranteeing 'total anonymity' to its financiers, was formed on 25 June 2010, eight days before the Commission was due to publish its investigation into TAB.[19] Donors to TAB seemed to have an unrelenting interest in keeping within Fox's line-of-sight, and continued to give to newly established Pargav – with Oliver Hylton as sole Director of the organisation (who acts as senior adviser to donor Hintze, notable donor to TAB).

The defence interests are obvious when confronted with the lists of names associated with The Atlantic Bridge. However, it was not only defence issues that were integral to TAB's point of interest, but also energy and health care. When Fox sat as Shadow Secretary of State for Health, he chaired a conference with TAB in May 2003 to discuss *'Scientific Research and Medical Provision: The Anglo-American Dynamic'*, which questioned the sustainability of the UK health care system, and what lessons we could learn from the US.[20] Attended by heads from the NHS, the Galen Institute (a US health and public policy lobbying group) and global pharmaceutical giants GlaxoSmithKline and Pfizer – it is all too tempting to interpret the purpose of these meetings and the intentions of those attending.

What we appear to have witnessed are the acts of international businesses seeking to exert influence and power, seemingly making use of Werritty's close connections with Fox, particularly as a number of those associated with The Atlantic Bridge had strong links to defence contractors (what parallels are there to the 'Arms-to-Iraq' affair of the 1980s?)

Attention has been diverted from Liam Fox and The Atlantic Bridge as news of Muammar Gaddafi's capture and subsequent death has swept across the globe. Prior to the 'triumph' of the West and its NATO forces, Fox's resignation speech started by acknowledging his recent challenging tasks in Libya, as he was confronted with *'an unbearable human tragedy'* on one hand, and a *'deep personal disappointment'* on the other (his resignation). Liam Fox: a man who could seemingly recognise a *'human tragedy'*, yet believed that *'for too many, peace has come to mean simply the absence of war. We cannot allow that corrosive view to go unchallenged'*.[21]

There is a second inquiry into the former Defence Minister by the Parliamentary Standards Commissioner who has accepted a complaint from John Mann MP about the use of Fox's Commons office to run The Atlantic Bridge.[22]

Notes

1 Report by the Cabinet Secretary Sir Gus O'Donnell, 'Allegations against Rt Hon Dr Liam Fox MP', 18 October 2011; Annex A - Letter from Ursula Brennan, Permanent Under-Secretary of State at Ministry of Defence to Sir Gus O'Donnell, 10 October 2011; Annex B - Occasions when Adam Werritty is known to have met with SOFS in main building and overseas travel

2 *Ibid* Para 22

3 Theo Usherwood, 'Liam Fox's Commons statement in full', *The Independent*, 19 October 2011

4 Winston Churchill, 'Sinews of Peace Address', Westminster College, Fulton, Missouri, March 1946 (speech)

5 Charity Commission Regulatory Case Report, The Atlantic Bridge Education and Research Scheme, Registered Charity Number 1099513

6 See *www.stephennewton.com/atlantic-bridge*

7 Amanda Bowman, 'What Britain's changing of the guard will mean for the US', *The Washington Examiner*, 7 April 2010

8 Charity Commission Regulatory Case Report, The Atlantic Bridge Education and Research Scheme, p6-7

9 Amnesty International UK, for example, has had to establish a separate Charitable Trust in order to carry out activities deemed charitable under UK legislation See *McGovern v Attorney-General [1982]*; *http://www.amnesty.org.uk/content.asp?CategoryID=10173*

10 See Wayback Machine (2008) *http://web.archive.org/web/20080522072502/http://www.theatlanticbridge.com/welcome.php* accessed 21/10/2011

11 *http://www.time.com/time/specials/packages/article/0,28804,1984685_1984864_1984901,00.htm* accessed 21/10/2011

12 *http://www.thehill.com/business-a-lobbying/138979-defense-industry-leiberman-will-be-hard-to-replace-* accessed 21/10/2011

13 Harry Hamburg, 'Giuliani: I'm one of "best known Americans"', *USA Today*, 19 September 2007

14 Rupert Neate, 'Liam Fox took five MPs to Washington with donor's money', *The Guardian*, 13 October 2011

15 Francis Elliott, 'Liam Fox accepted £50,000 from defence donor', *The Times*, 9 February 2010

16 *http://opencharities.org/charities/1099513* accessed 21/10/2011

17 Jamie Doward, 'Liam Fox's Atlantic Bridge linked top Tories and Tea Party Activists', *The Observer*, 15 October 2011

18 Andy McSmith, 'Hague forced to play down association with Werritty', *The Independent*, 17 October 2011

19 Jason Lewis, Robert Mendick and Patrick Hennessy, 'Fox affair: donors' fury over lies', *The Telegraph*, 15 October 2011

20 http://web.archive.org/web/20050331020013/www.theatlanticbridge.com/articles/ScienceConference.htm accessed 21/10/2011

21 *Ibid* (17) In a 2002 speech for TAB in New York

22 Andrew Grice, 'Fox faces a second inquiry as he turns his fire on media', *The Independent*, 20 October 2011

The Country and the City

Raymond Williams

Raymond Williams was a good friend to the Russell Foundation for many years, until his death in 1988. So Spokesman are very pleased indeed to bring back into print his landmark work, The Country and the City, *which Trevor Griffiths encouraged us to publish. To whet the appetite, we reprint an excerpt from chapter seven, which is entitled 'The Morality of Improvement'.*

At the same time, Parthian in Wales are publishing a new edition of The Long Revolution, *which first appeared 50 years ago in 1961. The Raymond Williams Society, and its journal* Key Words, *distributed by Spokesman, encourages us all by advancing Williams's influence on new generations.*

The true history of the English countryside has been centred throughout in the problems of property in land, and in the consequent social and working relationships. By the eighteenth century, nearly half of the cultivated land was owned by some five thousand families. As a central form of this predominance, four hundred families, in a population of some seven or eight million people, owned nearly a quarter of the cultivated land. Beneath this domination, there was no longer, in any classical sense, a peasantry, but an increasingly regular structure of tenant farmers and wage-labourers: the social relationships that we can properly call those of agrarian capitalism. The regulation of production was increasingly in terms of an organised market.

The transition from feudal and immediately post-feudal arrangements to this developing agrarian capitalism is of course immensely complicated. But its social implications are clear enough. It is true that the predominant landowning class was also, in political terms, an aristocracy, whose ancient or ancient-seeming titles and houses offered the illusion of a society determined by obligations and traditional relations between social orders. But the main activity of this class was of a radically different kind. They lived by a calculation of rents and returns on investments of capital, and it was the process of rack-renting, engrossing and enclosure which increased their hold on the land.

Yet there was never any simple confrontation between the four hundred families and a rural proletariat. On the contrary, between these poles of the economic process there was an increasingly stratified hierarchy of smaller landowners, large tenants, surviving small freeholders and copyholders, middle and small tenants, and cottagers and craftsmen with residual common rights. A process begun in the sixteenth century was still powerfully under way, with many of the smaller farms being suppressed, especially on improved arable land, while at the same time the area of cultivated land was itself steadily and at times dramatically increased. Even within the social relations of landowner, tenant, and labourer, there was a continual evolution of new attitudes. An estate passed from being regarded as an inheritance, carrying such and such income, to being calculated as an opportunity for investment, carrying greatly increased returns. In this development, an ideology of improvement – of a transformed and regulated land – became significant and directive. Social relations which stood in the way of this kind of modernisation were then steadily and at times ruthlessly broken down.

The crisis of values which resulted from these changes is enacted in varying ways in eighteenth-century literature. In poetry, as we shall see, the idealisation of the happy tenant, and of the rural retreat, gave way to a deep and melancholy consciousness of change and loss, which eventually established, in a new way, a conventional structure of retrospect.

But before this development, there was a lively engagement with the human consequences of the new institutions and emphases. Indeed it was in just this interest that the novel emerged as the most creative form of the time. The problems of love and marriage, in a society dominated by issues of property in land, were extended from the later Jacobean comedy and the Restoration comedy of manners, and from the moral epistles of Pope, to the novels of Richardson and Fielding, and in the mode of their extension were transformed. Allworthy and Squire Western, the neighbouring landowners in Fielding's *Tom Jones,* or Lovelace in Richardson's *Clarissa,* are in some ways lineal descendants of the world of Wellborn and Overreach, and then of Tunbelly Clumsey and Young Fashion. The plot of *Tom Jones* is based on the desire to link by marriage the two largest estates in Somersetshire: the proposed marriage of Sophia Western to Blifil is conceived for this end; her marriage to Tom Jones, when he is eventually revealed as Allworthy's true heir, achieves what had formerly, for personal reasons, been rejected. Similarly, Clarissa Harlowe's proposed marriage to Solmes is part of her family's calculation in concentrating their estates and increasing their rank; it is from this that she recoils to the destructive and cynical world of the established landowning aristocrat, Lovelace.

What is dramatised, under increasing pressure, in the actions of these novels, is the long process of choice between economic advantage and other ideas of value. Yet whereas, in the plays, we saw this from one particular standpoint – the social world of London in which the contracts were made and in which, by isolation and concentration, the tone of the protesting and then the cynical observer could be established and maintained – in the novels we move out to the families themselves, and see the action in its homes and in its private character. For all the differences between Richardson and Fielding, this change is something they have in common. Instead of the formal confrontation between representatives of different groups – the wellborn and the overreachers – and the amused observation of a distanced way of the world, the action becomes internal, and is experienced and dramatised as a problem of character.

The open ideology of improvement is in fact most apparent in Defoe, but in an abstraction which marks an essential difference from Richardson and Fielding. There is some irony in this fact, in that in his *Tour of England and Wales,* in the 1720s, Defoe was an incomparable observer of the detailed realities of country life, with his notes on methods of production, marketing and rents. It is from him that we learn the degree of specialisation and market-production in early eighteenth-century agriculture, and its intricate involvement with the cities, the ports, and the early coal, iron and cloth industrial areas. It is a frankly commercial world, with hardly any pastoral tinge, and Defoe's combination of intense interest and matter-of-fact reporting is the true predecessor of the major eighteenth-century tradition of rural inquiry, which runs on through William Marshall, the *County Reports,* Arthur Young and the Annals of Agriculture, to Cobbett and the nineteenth century. This emphasis is the real line of development of a working agriculture, and is in itself a major index of change. Yet, with rare exceptions, this emphasis was in its own way an abstraction from the social relationships and the human world through which the new methods of production worked. It is only at the end of this line, in the crisis at the turn of the century, that the social and economic inquiries are adequately brought together. It is then not surprising that Defoe, for all his close and specialised observation of what was happening in the fields and markets, did not, in his novels, consider their underlying social reality. Rather he projected, into other histories, the abstracted spirit of improvement and simple economic advantage – as most notably in *Robinson Crusoe* – and created a fictional world of isolated individuals to whom other people are basically transitory and functional – as again in *Crusoe* and in *Moll Flanders.* Consciously and unconsciously, this emphasis of a condition and of an ethic was prophetic and powerful; but it is an indication of its character that what Crusoe improves is a remote island, and that what Moll Flanders trades in is her own person. The important improvement and trading were at once nearer home and more general, but the simple practice and ethic of improvement could be more readily and more singlemindedly apprehended in deliberately isolated histories.

www.spokesmanbooks.com
www.raymondwilliams.co.uk
www.parthianbooks.com

* * *

Collier

He lies side on, man-foetus in the two-foot seam,
Half naked, hacking out the fires of ancient suns.
A mile above the laughing children dam the stream,
The hedges hang their flowers, the river runs.

Coiled in the Davy lamp dark he hews the coal, cuts
The black diamonds that power the dreadnought's screws,
That smelt the bullets' lead, that forge the iron boots
That police the Empire's bounds. Hunched

In the halo of the lamp's pale glow, curled,
Bent, he chops the boles of forests from a time
When giant lizards walked the world.
A mile above him in the summer sunlight

The rulers of a new world walk the links,
Gauge where their balls will fall. Belly-down, ink black
Below, the small man naked but for rags hacks on,
The weight of armies and empires on his back.

Mike Harding

Written earlier this year, after passing Agecroft where there was once a flourishing pit, the last in Manchester. Mike Harding's new book of poetry, Strange Lights Over Bexleyheath, *is published by Luath Press.*

www.mikeharding.co.uk
www.luath.co.uk

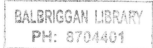

Reviews

Workers' Control

**Immanuel Ness and Dario Azzellini (eds), *Ours to Master and to Own:
Workers' Control from the Commune to the Present*, Haymarket, 444
pages, paperback ISBN 9781608461196, £13.99**

The editors are to be congratulated for bringing together a large number of
well-informed academics and activists from a dozen different countries to
make this a stimulating and challenging study.

What is workers' control? Can it be exercised in a capitalist society? If
so, in what way, and to what extent? How does it differ from self-
management? How might workers' control of individual enterprises and
self-management of industries be reconciled with the needs of consumers
and society as a whole? Are industries now too large and complex, and
workers too fragmented, for owners and managers to be effectively
controlled? Do workers struggling for control need the support of trade
unions and political parties? Is there a danger that the prejudices and
vested interests of politicians and officials will frustrate the aspirations of
working people?

These are some of the key questions for those of us who see the radical
expansion of industrial democracy as a crucial component for a just and
equal society. Many of these issues are vital elements that emerge in
various forms from the struggles, with their advances and defeats
recounted in these pages.

After a general historical and theoretical overview, the book moves
from the upheavals at the end of the Great War with factory committees
and factory councils emerging in Russia, Germany and Italy, through the
less known experience of the workers' committees in the Spanish
revolution to the experience of self-management in Yugoslavia and the
struggle for greater workers' power in communist Poland. There follow
accounts of workers' control developments as part of the anti-colonial
struggles after the Second World War in Indonesia and Algeria, and in the
resistance to dictatorship in Argentina and Portugal. More recent
developments in India, Venezuela and Brazil demonstrate that the 'big
flame' is still very much alight.

The Big Flame was a play directed by Ken Loach about the occupation
of their workplace by Liverpool dockers. It is referred to by Alan Tuckman
in his well-researched chapter on the politics of factory occupations in

Britain in the 1970s. The drama was first shown on television in 1969 and presaged the work-in at the Upper Clyde Shipyards (UCS) which was followed by a whole rash of sit-ins and work-ins. These arose from the spontaneous actions of groups of workers whose jobs were under threat. The Institute for Workers' Control (IWC – formed in 1968 after a series of industry and national conferences), did all it could to support and publicise these actions, but there was no central direction or co-ordination.

What happened in Britain is almost a model of the common ingredients needed to generate the surges in workers' control, many of the successes and failures of which are portrayed in these pages. They seem to require the interaction between crisis in the economy and society and its institutions, instability of the governing class, with the reaction of working people to the consequent pressure on their livelihoods, and the feeding of all these phenomena into the political process. Here the imposition of rationalisation, closures and redundancies in the face of technological change and growing competition in the market produced desperate but imaginative reactions from workforces under threat, where standard trade union responses were inadequate. Tony Benn, in opposition, gave prominent support to the UCS work-in and promised funds when in government for the worker co-operatives which arose from resistance to the cutbacks at places such as Fisher-Bendix, Triumph Meriden, the Scottish Daily News and, later, Imperial Typewriters.

It was in this context that the Labour Party developed its radical alternative economic strategy. This involved major intervention in the economy and included the promotion of public enterprise and industrial democracy through the creation of a national enterprise board in which trade unions and shop stewards would have strong representation. In addition, it proposed to set up planning agreements with major multinational companies on which trade unionists would have similar representation.

But this policy was not at all to the liking of Premier Wilson or his successor, James Callaghan. After giving great encouragement to shop stewards and workers' initiatives, in the face of intense pressure from industrialists and regular outcries from their friends in the media, Benn was sidelined by Wilson from the Industry Department to Energy in 1975. When the sterling crisis broke in 1976, Callaghan's government caved in to the restrictive demands of the International Monetary Fund, and the party's radical plans were either neutered or quietly dropped. Funds for the 'Benn Co-ops', such as they were, dried up. Some staggered on but with small impact either on the economy or as a focus for people's hopes and aspirations. In this climate there were but few attempts by workers in dispute to repeat the occupation tactic.

This history illustrates clearly how industrial and political activity, involving trade unionists and shop stewards, politicians and activists, are entwined and are essential to reinforce one another, working in the same direction, if they are to succeed. But the persistence and resources of the established order has always made such unity difficult to sustain. The major economic and environmental crises now encompassing the globe mean that co-ordinated resistance is all the more necessary, but that much more difficult because it requires action on an international scale.

This a daunting challenge, but the title of this book reminds me of the powerful words of William Morris; 'No man is good enough to be another man's master'. Ken Coates, the leading British protagonist for workers' control, had them inscribed on the IWC banner. I am sure he would say that as long as people refuse to submit to the whims and wishes of the powerful few then they will find together in themselves the ingenuity and means to resist and, sometimes, to prevail.

Today, the 'masters' are more difficult to confront because they are disguised in the form of huge remote institutions. Yet the impulse to insist on democratic accountability is stronger than ever. Interestingly, its most recent and powerful manifestation has been in the occupations of business premises of those powerful multinationals that are deemed to be responsible for the current grave economic crisis. It is a great encouragement that, despite all the obstacles, disappointments and failures, the past can be reinvented in many new and imaginative ways.

Ken Fleet
Secretary of the Institute for Workers' Control for many years

Economic Genocide

Naomi Klein, *The Shock Doctrine: The Rise of Disaster Capitalism*, Penguin 2008, 576 pages, paperback ISBN 9780141024530, £12.99

I simply do not understand how I could have missed this exceedingly important book when it first came out in 2007. I only bought it now because my niece got arrested at a demonstration in Washington along with Naomi Klein, and told me to read *The Shock Doctrine*. It is a riveting and most thoroughly researched account of the whole 'neo-liberal' globalisation process, which the world has suffered during the last four decades since the 1970s. I knew, as we all did, that the collapse of the Soviet Union had made possible the opening up of inequalities in capitalist development, which

Reagan and Thatcher had exploited to provide the chance this gave them to introduce their reactionary policies – with a little help from the Falklands War. I knew that Milton Friedman and his 'Chicago School' had been involved in the overthrow of Allende, and in the coup which established Pinochet's dictatorship in Chile, in 1973. But three things I did not know, and have learnt from Naomi Klein, which are truly shocking. The first thing she tells is of the deep involvement of Friedman and 'The Chicago Boys', not only in Chile, but in establishing the other Latin American dictatorships, and in counter-revolution in Russia, Eastern Europe, China, Iraq, South Africa and elsewhere – especially Iraq. Donald Rumsfeld, who attended Friedman's seminar in the 1960s, described the 'Chicago Boys' as 'a cluster of geniuses'. The second lesson for me is of the deliberate encouragement of 'shock' by the United States, as in 'shock and awe' in the Iraq war and elsewhere, as a sort of shock therapy, clearing the way in people's minds for 'neo-liberal' measures. Finally, there comes the most shocking revelation of all, the deliberate use of kidnapping and murder – an estimated 300 academics in Iraq – and of torture as a method, not of revealing secrets, but of erasing previously held convictions in populations being subjected to counter-revolutionary measures.

Milton Friedman's Chicago School prescription for remedying the world's economic ills, and for which he was awarded the Nobel Prize, consisted of three measures, accepted by the International Monetary Fund and the World Bank as the 'Washington Consensus': deregulation, that is of national financial controls; privatisation of nation state activities, especially 'Welfare State'; and general cut-backs in state spending. To achieve these aims, it was necessary to reduce the power of trade unions and other social organisations, ending what Thatcher called 'Society', and leaving all economic activity to individuals and families bargaining in a supposedly 'free' market. The different levels of power in the hands of those individuals was not examined, but was made more than ever unequal in such a 'free for all'.

Naomi Klein's detailed studies of successive counter-revolutions, in the sense of the reversal of hard-won freedoms for ordinary people, make for an extraordinary picture – in Chile, Argentina, Uruguay, Bolivia, Indonesia, Poland, Russia, China, South Africa, Iraq. The Chinese Mandarin for 'crisis' is danger plus opportunity, and this is Naomi Klein's explanation of the 'shock doctrine'. The opportunity which follows the critical shock is taken by the few with power in reordering the lives of the powerless many. In a speech in America, reported in *The Guardian* on 8 October 2011, Naomi Klein distinguishes the 'few' as 1% and the rest of us as 99%. Whatever the numbers, the task in her view of the few is nothing less than 'changing the underlying values of our society'. Now, that was what Friedman sought to do in his Chicago School – ending the search for co-operative social provision to meet human needs, supported by state regulation and restriction of private initiative, and replacing this with the freeing up of private enterprise in open markets for goods and services, supported by the widest possible global competition. It can hardly have escaped the notice of even the most enthusiastic individualists among the Chicago School that some – a very few – have immensely greater power than the many, and that this basic inequality has been steadily widening over the last forty years. What they might or might not admit is that much of the widening has been due to the introduction of Friedmanite measures all over the world. They would justify this on the bold assumption that it is the few, Chicago Boys included, who are responsible for all the invention and innovation that has made lives so much easier – for some of us, at others' expense.

The shocks of the 'Shock Doctrine' which Naomi Klein studies in such detail involve many different kinds of crisis, and they are not necessarily deliberately engineered by the powerful few. The 'Shock and Awe' of the Iraq War was a special case, and was a signal failure, as Naomi Klein's account reveals, in producing, as intended, a change of mindset among Iraqis favourable to US effective control of the oil supplies, let alone better living conditions for the many. US contractors such as Vice-President Cheney's Haliburton and the giant US armament companies made enormous profits. The actual results inside Iraq, apart from the devastation of power and water supplies and health services, was the exacerbation of ethnic and religious differences between Sunnis and Shias, and between them and the Kurds, and the deliberate use of murder and torture to control popular resistance.

The Iraq War was perhaps a special case, supposedly justified as a response to the Al Qaeda destruction of New York's twin towers and other targets on the infamous 9/11 attacks, but quite evidently the excuse for the real 'shock doctrine'. Other wars which provided the opportunity for shock treatment were Mrs Thatcher's Falklands War, Russia's war with Chechnya, the Tamil Tigers' war in Sri Lanka, and civil wars in the Sudan, the Congo and South Africa. Military coups were no less valuable opportunities than actual wars for Friedmanite reconstruction. US support for shock therapy in the collapsing Soviet Union was remarkable, including not only the destruction of Solidarity in Poland but also of Gorbachev in the Yeltsin coup in Russia. The only difference from the usual pattern in the 'Shock Doctrine' being that Russian oligarchs and not American ones picked up the bits – but they were big bits. Similarly in China, which Friedman visited in his old age, the chief beneficiaries of the crackdown in Tiananmen Square were the Chinese élite. As always, the masses suffered. Naomi Klein reveals two astonishing facts about 'shock doctrine' in Russia and Asia: first, that after the Yeltsin coup in 1993, 600,000 more people moved from ex-Soviet states to Israel, solving Israel's problems of both labouring masses and skilled technicians; second, Stanley Fischer, 'chief architect of the IMF's shock therapy adventures in Russia and Asia', became Israel's new Central Bank chief. Perhaps it is not surprising that Israel is one of the world's largest arms dealers.

After Pinochet in Chile, the military Junta in Argentina, and dictatorship in Uruguay, Bolivia and Nicaragua were all financed by the US and 'liberalised' by Friedman. After Chile, the main Latin American crises were due to rising debts and runaway inflation. One specialty American shock was the 'Volcker shock', after the US Federal Reserve Chairman, Paul Volcker, in 1981 raised US interest rates to 21%, thereby greatly increasing the debt burden. It can hardly be said that Friedmanite policies cured these diseases, but after some decades, as Naomi Klein makes clear, Latin Americans began to get over the shock and the unpaid debts they were left with, and to get fed up with dictators and gross inequalities, especially between the white and coloured populations, and look for governments committed to a reconstruction that is more protective of the many poor, and less of the few rich.

One crisis Naomi Klein includes in her list of shocks is natural disaster. The flooding of New Orleans, Hurricane Mitch in Honduras, and the Indonesian tsunami, not to mention the BP oil disaster in the Bay of Mexico, became famous for the resultant neglect of the people who suffered most and for the attention to reviving these coastal areas for tourism.

Naomi Klein's book ends in 2007. Since then, we have had the most serious financial and economic crisis since the 1930s, plus continuing war in Afghanistan, a new war in Libya, repression in Syria and Yemen, and further Israeli attacks on Palestine. What would Naomi Klein be saying now? It is too early to judge how all these shocks will be resolved. The Arab revolt in Tunisia seemed to create an opening for democracy. The revolt in Egypt seems less likely to lead to a democratic solution, and the shocks in the rest of the Arab world hardly look like benefiting their peoples. What is sure is that the West will hold on to its control of Libya's oil. Whatever the aims of the Libyan people, and its fighters, it was that control which Gaddafi was challenging, and to stop him the reason for the need for NATO support of the Libyan rebels. What we can see in the UK today, and to some extent in the European Union, is the most remarkable protection for the very rich, and for the bankers in particular, while all the rest of us and, particularly, the poorest are made to pay for the crisis in what is called a freeing up of the market. This is pure Friedman Chicago School economics, which will only serve to deepen and prolong the slump. The protests of the British and other peoples remain our only hope of moving towards a reconstruction that is both just and sustainable.

Michael Barratt Brown

Chavs

Owen Jones, *Chavs: The Demonization of the Working Class*, **Verso, 2011, 298 pages, paperback, ISBN 9781844676965, £14.99**

Given the recent outbreaks of rioting and looting in London and other major cities, this book could not be more prescient. If, unlike Boris Johnson and David Cameron, you do believe the disturbances to have a fundamentally different explanation which does not primarily highlight 'pure criminality' then this book will undoubtedly bolster your opinion. Rioting, as Martin Luther King perceptively opined, is a manifestation of the 'voice of the unheard', and the recent occurrences are certainly no exception. The author uses the concept of the 'Chav' to explain why the working class has become largely politically neutered, if not voiceless, over the last 30 years. He uses the question of the stigmatisation of a section of the working class to describe and comment on the problems facing the Left after years of political defeats.

The definition of a 'chav' ranges from the most neutral in the *Collins English Dictionary* (2005), 'a young working-class person who dresses in casual sports clothing', to the 'feral underclass' of the ex-*Daily Telegraph* journalist Simon Heffer and, ultimately, to the ravings of reader opinions on the *Daily Mail* website depicting 'tattooed, loud, foul-mouthed proles, with scummy brats'. Then there are television programmes which ram home the message of a debased and depraved sub-proletariat inhabiting (usually) council estates. Of particular resonance are the programme *Shameless* and the characters Wayne and Waynetta Slob in Harry Enfield's repertory of characters, not forgetting Little Britain's comic efforts. Other examples in the book are a gym club that includes in its activities 'Chav Fighting' and holiday companies which advertises their holiday packages as 'Chav-Free'. Naturally, the internet provides innumerable 'chav' hating web sites. What these various concepts of a 'chav' seek to represent is a working-class person, often unemployed, ill-educated, work-shy, potentially violent, living on benefits, and drug and/or alcohol dependent. Furthermore, if she is female then she is promiscuous, usually a single mother with several children, and living in social housing. A further confirmation of these attitudes is to be found in the first chapter where the author contrasts the initial media treatment of the tragedy of an abducted child, comparing the cases of Shannon Matthews and Madeleine McCann. The shabby journalistic treatment of Shannon and the subsequent reinforcement of stereotypical attitudes towards the people living in the Dewsbury Moor council estate are described in detail.

The author's thesis regarding the present situation of the working class takes us into the only too familiar territory of political defeats and decline of the Left over the last 30 years. The assault on the working class started with the 'creative destruction' of a large portion of manufacturing, extractive and heavy industries, through the deliberate deflationary policies adopted by the Thatcher administration. This conscious manoeuvre released the weapon of mass unemployment which, coupled with anti-union laws, depleted both the membership and the defensive power of the unions. Meanwhile, much of the industrial proletariat was being re-constituted in various Third World countries as multinational companies moved production to where wage costs were lower.

Jones argues that the diminution of trade union power and membership coupled with the Labour Party's failure to adopt a posture of united defiance against Thatcherism, illustrated by the formation of the SDP and the failure of the party leadership to support the miners' strike, were major factors in ensuring successive Labour electoral defeats. This engendered a party so desperate for electoral success that it swallowed Kinnock's drift to the right and, after the interregnum of John Smith, succumbed to the blandishments of New Labour. With the abandonment of Clause Four and assurances to the élite that they were 'relaxed' about the filthy rich getting richer, New Labour was ready for office and we are all too well aware of the path chosen by Blair and Brown in government.

Jones aptly states that 'if New Labour had an official religion, it would surely be meritocracy ...', but concentrating on equality of opportunity rather than equality of condition. Britain now has 13.5 million people in poverty. De-industrialisation has seen Nottingham, for example, formerly a centre of light engineering, mining, pharmaceuticals and the hosiery industry, reach such a state that, by 2010, 31.6 per cent of its households were workless according to the Office of National Statistics (*Guardian* 09/09/11). The level playing field, so beloved of all those who try to convince us that 'we are all middle class now', has a decided slope, and the book devotes a chapter to puncturing such outright nonsense. Small wonder that elements of the working class, ignored by New Labour, sought solace in the British National Party, and Jones devotes an insightful chapter entitled 'Backlash' to this phenomenon.

The author has been criticised for a tendency to idealise working-class attitudes and community cohesion prior to Thatcherism, but there is surely more than a grain of truth in his statement that 'old working-class values, like solidarity, were replaced by dog-eat-dog individualism'. He makes an eloquent case that this kind of abrasive selfishness as a philosophy has to be sustained by a combination of class hatred, distorted meritocratic arguments, economic obfuscation, and the assertion that there is an inherent lack of aspirational drive within this section of society owing to the state's feather-bedding in the form of over-generous benefits. However, the author perhaps does not take into account sufficiently that the working class is more segmented than he allows for, and that the suffering amongst working-class communities was not uniformly spread. In fact, 'chav' hating is not something confined to the middle class and the élite, but segments of the prosperous and 'respectable' working class also have a far from sympathetic attitude to the poor despite the reality of their hardship. These attitudes, of course, are fed by the media, but are helped by the social segregation implicit in now utilising council housing as 'transit camps for the needy'. This is a far cry from the hopes of Aneurin Bevan that council housing would have the social mix associated with the 'English and Welsh villages, where the doctor, the grocer, the butcher and the farm labourer all lived on the same street'. The right-to-buy and the supposed, but now increasingly dubious, asset of home ownership have undoubtedly assisted the divisions within the working class.

The author is an Oxford history graduate from Stockport and used to work as a trade union parliamentary researcher, so apart from anything else the book is factually highly informative. His conversations with the likes of Geoffrey Howe and Stephen Byers provide useful illustrations of the book's argument. Particularly piquant is his chat with Rachel Johnson, editor of *The Lady* and sister of the archetypal old Etonian and Bullingdon Club rowdy, Boris Johnson. The book exudes the youthful verve and enthusiasm of Jones for resuscitating the Labour Movement and, although he does not advance a comprehensive programme, he is surely right when he says such a renewal must be based on the struggle against structural unemployment and the fight for decent jobs. By 'decent' he obviously means jobs that provide security and a living wage, but more consideration needs to be shown to the changed nature of industry since the 1970s, and in this context to address the necessity of a reduction in working hours.

In the conclusion Jones pointedly raises the situation of the Labour Party's reduction in working-class electoral support, demonstrated by the loss of five million voters, four million of whom were lost under Blair's premiership. He questions what Labour's response should be to what Ed Miliband himself has called 'a crisis of working-class representation'. Unfortunately, the latter's speech at the Trade Union Congress in September 2011 is not the kind of response that is at all helpful. The Coalition Government, in reality, wishes to dwarf Thatcher's achievements by drastic reductions in state welfare provisions, creating the neo-liberal 'minimalist state', and privatising its residue. They have an agenda which, having deftly shifted the reasons for the economic crisis onto Labour, away from their banking compatriots in the City, now seeks to make the working class pay for the crisis. They are determined ideologues with a radical class-war-based agenda, to whom the demonization of the working class provides a helpfully divisive smoke screen to mask their intentions. The author wants to engender a return to the politics of class and 'at least build a counterweight to the hegemonic, unchallenged class politics of the wealthy'. What is needed is a counter class consciousness to match that of the élite, and this book should help to realise that ambition. *Chavs* is written in a clear, non-academic style, and is the ideal book to explain how we arrived at the present lamentable situation. It should enthuse a new generation of prospective activists.

John Daniels

Mixed Economy?

Ha-Joon Chang, *Bad Samaritans: The Guilty Secrets of Rich Nations and The Threat to Global Prosperity*, Random House, 2007, 266 pages, paperback ISBN 9781905211371, £8.99

Commenting on the work of the (South Korean) Cambridge University economist Ha-Joon Chang, Martin Wolf in the *Financial Times* engaged in typical neo-liberal newspeak, describing Chang as 'probably the world's most effective critic of globalization'. He is nothing of the sort, but a fierce opponent of neo-liberal dogmas instead. His book *Bad Samaritans* is a finely tuned demolition job, set against many of the myths carefully inculcated by mainstream politics, the mass media and orthodox academic circles over several recent decades.

Chang's account, rich in factual detail and empirical support, ripostes to most of the basic popular preconceptions surrounding the 'free market' policies advanced by global and national political and economic élites. It systematically demonstrates how the turbo-capitalist, 'one-size fits all' mantras of 'privatisation, deregulation and liberalisation' (along with low inflation, balancing of the budget, etc.) – continually imposed on developing countries by the Western élites and their compradorial partners in the satellite, client states – do not have much credibility as far as needs for economic development and social progress are concerned. Instead, these policies aim to pull developing and transitional economies into rich countries' (and, more directly, rich companies') accumulation cycles, stifling their own endogenous resources and potentials.

In the world of global economic governance plutocracy has replaced democracy, and the one-dollar-one-vote system means that the rich countries control 60% of voting shares in the IMF and the World Bank. The World Trade Organisation is nominally democratic (China and Luxemburg have the same number of votes), but Chang observes that it is effectively run by an oligarchy of richest countries, and that crucial ministerial meetings (such as the ones in Geneva in 1998, in Seattle in 1999, in Doha in 2001, and in Cancun in 2003) were held on a 'by-invitation-only' basis in so-called Green Rooms. Mafia style, some delegates from developing countries who tried to attend these closed meetings were even physically thrown out. Chang points out that threats and bribery in international economic negotiations are also commonplace. In the most literal sense, the game is rigged.

The neo-liberal agenda-setters, in powerful and weak countries alike, typically point to the rise of the 'Asian tigers' as an example of neo-liberal efficiency, its economic and social superiority. The reality was in many ways diametrically opposed to this propaganda. Chang emphasises how South Korea, represented as a neo-liberal prodigy, tenaciously employed measures such as tariff protection, subsidies and other forms of state support in order to foster and shield some industries (which were selected by the government in conjunction with the private sector), until they could withstand foreign competition. The state also retained possession of the entire banking sector, unapologetically (and pragmatically) setting up state-owned enterprises and taking over private companies if they were mismanaged. Taiwan, China, India and others also made use of similar forms of state intervention. Even Chile, sometimes hailed as the most illustrious example of neo-liberal success (after the CIA-sponsored coup against the democratically elected socialist government of Salvador Allende), took on a much more interventionist attitude after its financial crash of 1982, when it nationalised its entire banking sector, which was followed by the allocation of significant state support to private companies in overseas marketing and R&D, the introduction of capital controls to combat short-term speculative funds in the 1990s, and so on.

Chang is also illuminating on the question of state ownership, which is the central anathema of 'free market' capitalists. He points out that '(t)he economic successes of many European economies, such as Austria, Finland, France, Norway and Italy after the Second World War, were achieved with very large SOE [state-owned enterprise] sectors at least until the 1980s. In Finland and France especially, the SOE sector was at the forefront of technological modernization' (p. 110). Very large SOE sectors still exist in 'Asian tigers' such as China, Taiwan, and indeed the famed, supposedly 'neo-liberal' Singapore, whose state-owned sector is twice the size of Korea's, which is significant as well. Chang manages to grasp the anti-democratic content which is at the heart of demands for reduced governmental involvement in the economy – privatisation and 'liberalisation' aim to minimise scope for policy discretion.

> 'Democracy is acceptable to neo-liberals only in so far as it does not contradict the free market; this is why some of them saw no contradiction between supporting the Pinochet dictatorship and praising democracy ... (U)nlike their intellectual predecessors, neo-liberals live in an era when they cannot openly oppose democracy, so they try to do it by discrediting *politics in general*. By discrediting politics in general, they gain legitimacy for their actions that take away decision powers from the democratically elected representatives. In doing so, neo-liberals have succeeded in diminishing the scope for democratic control without ever openly criticising democracy itself' (p. 176).

In the same key, he observes one of the strategic aims behind the neo-liberal emphasis on 'depoliticised', rigid monetary and fiscal policies aimed at lowering inflation: they also diminish room for policy intervention, helping to inaugurate and preserve the independence of national central banks from the state, and from any form of democratic accountability. Chang does not deny the negativities of high inflation, but seeks to demonstrate how moderate inflation can actually be congruent with accelerated economic growth, and argues that positive aspects of low inflation are often counterbalanced by the reduction of workers' future earnings through reduced growth, reduced employment prospects and reduced wage rates (on the other hand, financial industry benefits from low inflation, as its profits depend on financial assets with fixed returns).

Chang puts monetarist arguments to the test by documenting certain cases in which a glaring absence of correlation between prosperity and anti-inflationist policies can be observed. For instance, Brazil's average inflation rate in the 1960s and 70s was 42%, yet the country's *per capita* income grew annually by 4,5% in this period. Conversely, the growth in its *per capita* income was sharply reduced when its inflation rate was lowered. South

Korea's development tells a similar story. These perplexing cases (from the vantage point of official monetarist dogma) demonstrate that the richest countries do not maintain their monetarist prescriptions out of altruism for developing countries, but rather to erode developmental strategies which favour investment, demand management and growth. Developing countries, which need to accelerate growth, investments and jobs most, are therefore often forced by the IMF to balance their budgets every year. As usual with neo-liberalism, double standards reign supreme. Instead of following their own advice, which they present to developing countries, rich and powerful countries regularly reduce their own interest rates and increase state deficits in order to stimulate economic demand. 'When Korea was in its biggest-ever financial crisis in 1997, the IMF allowed the country to run budget deficits equivalent to only 0,8% of GDP (and, at that, after trying the opposite for several months, with disastrous consequences); when Sweden had a similar problem (due to the ill-managed opening-up of its capital market, as was the case with Korea in 1997) in the early 1990s, its budget deficits were, in proportional terms, ten times that (8% of its GDP)' (pp. 158-9). Even the administration of a fervent 'free marketer' such as George W. Bush engaged in extensive deficit spending (and, one might add, the present recession helps reveal just how extravagantly detached most leading capitalist metropoles were from their own recipes of 'fiscal prudence').

In addition to its failure in delivering equality and growth, the implementation of neo-liberal doctrine has failed to bring economic (and social) security and stability. Instead, as Chang pointed out (even before the latest crisis), '(t)he world, especially the developing world, has seen more frequent and larger-scale financial crises since the 1980s' (p.28). The post-WWII Keynesian 'golden age' of state-led industrialisation, brought about as a result of the anti-colonial, democratic and socialist tectonic shifts in global politics, had led to historic social and economic advances: 'During the period of controlled globalization underpinned by nationalistic policies between the 1950s and the 1970s, the world economy, especially in the developing world, was growing faster, was more stable and had more equitable income distribution than in the past two and a half decades of rapid and uncontrolled neo-liberal globalization.'

In contrast to the received wisdom of recent decades, post-WWII development of poor nations didn't fundamentally conflict with the welfare and stability of Western societies. The corrective influence of Cold War positioning on the behaviour of the US and other Western powers, and especially the assertiveness of decolonising and developing countries, meant that the less developed economies were to a large degree allowed to pursue policies which protected their nascent industries. Mostly as a result of this (relatively non-dogmatic) planning in numerous developing as well as developed countries, the period between 1950-1973 was characterised by rising standards of living worldwide. '*Per capita* income growth rate shot up from 1,3% in the liberal golden age (1870-1913) to 4.1% in Europe ... These spectacular growth performances were combined with low income inequality and economic stability'. The *per capita* income in developing countries grew at 'twice the rate they have recorded since the 1980s under neo-liberal policies'.

Chang's work is a brilliant call for strategic openness, a resolute negation of the mantra that there is no alternative. Unlike many quasi-Keynesian opportunists, he does not gloss over the potential for widespread corruption through deregulation and privatisation: 'Deregulation of the economy in general, and the introduction of greater market forces in the management of the government more specifically, has often increased, rather than reduced, corruption' (p. 180). He bluntly states that 'privatization ... can be a recipe for disaster, especially in developing countries that lack the necessary regulatory capabilities' (p. 119), as well as that '(s)ome of the world's best firms are owned and run by the state' (pp. 17-18). Still, progressive as these arguments and assertions are in the present situation, Chang also devoted the latter part of his book to deepening his critique of some of the fundamental structural defects in the present socio-economic system. A progressive technocratic critique of neo-liberalism is often as far as heterodox economists are currently willing to go. Commendably, Chang goes further to uncover some basic issues regarding social and economic democratisation. He recognises that 'market and democracy clash at a fundamental level. Democracy runs the principle of "one man (one person), one vote". The market runs on the principle of "one dollar, one vote". Naturally, the former gives equal weight to each person, regardless of the money she/he has. The latter gives greater weight to richer people. Therefore, democratic decisions usually subvert the logic of the market' (p. 172).

Yet, despite this valiant step, his open-mindedness towards state ownership does not also result in a sufficiently sustained attempt to consider genuinely public, democratic and co-operative forms of ownership. Even in his latest (also brilliant) book, *23 Things They Don't Tell You About Capitalism* (Penguin Books, 2010 – see *Spokesman 111*), which broadens and in some respects deepens the arguments made in *Bad Samaritans*, Chang could have discussed the subject of workplace democracy at more length. In this latest book, his position on workplace democracy is refreshingly progressive, yet he doesn't give it quite the attention it deserves. Thus he fails to emphasise (for instance) the work of the 2009 Nobel Laureate in Economics, Elinor Ostrom, who has shown that social ownership is in fact more efficient in the management of public resources than both private and state ownership. None the less, Chang (as well as some of the more 'mainstream' critical economists, such as Stiglitz and Krugman) helps to carve out a discursive terrain more amenable to radical critiques of capitalism. It is the task of the democratic Left to take advantage of this new space and plant ideas and arguments that will advance an authentic political, economic and social democracy.

Daniel Jakopovich

Looking Back

Kenneth O. Morgan, *Ages of Reform: Dawns and Downfalls of the British Left*, I.B.Taurus, 2011, 320 pages, hardback ISBN 978184885 5762, £27.50

Kenneth O. Morgan is a distinguished historian of the Left in Britain, who has written more than thirty books including biographies of James Callaghan and Michael Foot. This book consists of a series of essays dealing with events, episodes and individuals connected with developments on the Left of the political spectrum over the last two centuries. Versions of most of these have already appeared elsewhere and they reflect the views of the author, who has been a member of the Labour Party since 1955 and a member of the House of Lords since 2001.

He begins with the 1832 Reform Act, which abolished the worst features of the pre-existing electoral system – the rotten boroughs – in which a handful of voters were controlled by the landowners and returned over fifty Members of Parliament. As he points out, however, although a massive step forward, the Act retained a property qualification for voters and can by no means be regarded as establishing democracy in Britain.

He devotes a chapter to W. E. Gladstone, four times a Liberal Prime Minister, and evaluates his great contribution to the creation and development of the Liberal Party. This is a prelude to his dissertations on David Lloyd George, the paradoxes in whose career he brings out. How did a 'little England' opponent of the Boer War become the all-powerful British leader in the First World War, and then an advocate of appeasement and compromise with Hitler in the 1930s and 40s? Morgan is anxious to rehabilitate Lloyd George's reputation by referring to his progressive role in the 1906-14 Liberal Government, and by drawing attention to his unhappiness about the harsh terms imposed upon Germany by the Treaty of Versailles, which many now regard as a factor contributing to the rise of Nazism.

Morgan compares the progressive movements in Britain and the United States. He points out that although the International Workers of the World (the Wobblies) and Daniel de Leon excited some interest on the Left in Britain, trade union-led struggles in Britain – particularly the great unrest before the First World War – tended to alienate American progressives.

When he comes to consider the development of the British Labour Party over the years since its foundation in 1900, Morgan traces the key role played by socialist ideas until the advent to power of Tony Blair and New Labour. He emphasises the fact that Hugh Gaitskell, Anthony Crosland, Roy Jenkins, James Callaghan and Harold Wilson all regarded themselves as socialists, although the meaning they attached to this description of themselves varied. He enumerates seven ages of socialism from the period of James Keir Hardie, when it was a gospel of fraternity, down to the rejection of Clause IV and its replacement by various vague doctrines like that of the 'Third Way'. He points out that there has not been any significant new statement of the meaning of socialism since Anthony Crosland's book, *The Future of Socialism*, and considers that Michael Foot and Tony Benn both lost their versions in Labour's 1983 General Election defeat.

His chapter on the rise and fall of nationalisation suggests that, although inseparable from socialist ideas in the past, after 1983 Labour turned its back on the idea. In all this, Morgan fails to bring out that the privatised industries are far from being a great success. Just, as he notes, the Labour Government was virtually obliged to nationalise Northern Rock, Bradford & Bingley, the Royal Bank of Scotland, etc., albeit as a temporary measure – the growing economic crisis and other developments may well make renationalisation of privatised industries a realistic and desirable option in the future. The railways, to take one example, are less efficient and require a bigger subsidy – part of which goes in dividends to shareholders – than was the case when they were owned and operated by British Rail.

One of Morgan's chapters deals with imperialism. He gives considerable credit to the Fabian Colonial Research Bureau, but dismisses the work of the Movement for Colonial Freedom in campaigning for decolonisation as of little importance. 'The anti-imperialist rhetoric of the MCF was marginalised' [p.177]. As the Chair and, subsequently, the President of MCF, I have a different view of its effectiveness. However, he concedes that Harold Wilson, Anthony Greenwood and Barbara Castle – together with other ministers in the 1964-70 Labour Government – were former MCF members, and he praises Labour for granting self-government to the colonies without much more bloodshed:

> 'The ending of empire, even with difficult problems remaining in Cyprus and Rhodesia, was in many ways Old Labour's greatest moral victory' [p.180].

Morgan devotes a number of chapters to key Labour Party personalities. He praises Hugh Gaitskell, whom he twice met, and considers that Michael Foot's two-volume biography of Aneurin Bevan is grossly unfair to the former. He argues that Bevan was essentially a middle of the road figure and not a left-winger except on some aspects of foreign policy in the 1950s.

Michael Foot and the Bevanites were far more anti-Gaitskell than Bevan, he contends. Michael Foot was a great communicator, orator and journalist and an outstanding man of letters. He was not, in Morgan's judgment, however, temperamentally or psychologically equipped to lead the Labour Party and his 1983 campaign was pathetic. Morgan gives him credit for the role he played supporting the Labour Governments of 1974-79, but he does not fully recognise his achievement in 1980/83 in holding the Labour Party together in the face of the activities of the Gang of Four and the SDP on the right, and those on the Left who wrongly judged that their time had come.

One very positive service which this book performs, in the chapter headed 'Was Britain Dying?', is to counter the propaganda of the Conservatives and New Labour that the Wilson-Callaghan period of 1974-79 was solely characterised by sleaze, strikes and economic decline. Morgan brings out the economic successes, restoring Britain after the three-day week and the miners' strike, countering the inflationary pressures produced by the uplift in oil prices, the improvement achieved after the 1976 IMF crisis, when economic forecasts were appalling, and the fact that the commitments to the public services, to greater social and racial equality, and reducing unemployment were maintained.

As a back-bench Labour MP at that time, I had numerous criticisms of the Government's policies, but they were never those of the Conservatives or those who believed in abandoning our socialist ideals.

Morgan was a member of a group of republican peers in 2002 and is critical of the Labour Party for its failure to adopt a more anti-royalist approach. In the face of the weight of public opinion over many years and at the present time, however, it is hardly surprising that the abolition of the monarchy has been relegated to a very low priority.

The essays of which this book is comprised are of interest to those concerned with the development of the Left in Britain but they are hardly for beginners. The topics selected by the author are not linked by an underlying continuing theme but comprise a selection of issues on which the author has strong personal views.

His final chapter is on the Iraq War, on which he believes there was a gulf between the Labour Government and the British people. He analyses this at some length and expresses deep concern over the resultant loss of many good members from the Labour Party. Tony Blair, he says, should be wary about not becoming another Ramsay MacDonald. Many of us consider, however, that he has already done more damage to the Party than MacDonald did.

In so far as this book helps us to understand more fully a mix of episodes in the history of the progressive movement in Britain, it fulfils a useful role. It is not, however, a history of the British Left, and some of the author's conclusions are controversial.

Stan Newens

Palestine

Ali Abunimah, *One Country: A Bold Proposal to End the Israeli-Palestinian Impasse*, Holt McDougal, 2007, 240 pages, ISBN 9780805086669, £10.43

As the title concisely suggests, Ali Abunimah's book advocates a solution to the Arab-Israeli conflict based on the creation of one state in all of historic Palestine.

He bases his argument on three main points. The first is that the two-state solution, supported by virtually all governments involved in the struggle, is doomed to failure. The second is that the aspirations of Israeli Jews as well as Arab Palestinians can be realized in a single state in historic Palestine. The third is that it is possible for Israelis and Palestinians to unite under such a state.

On the first point, Abunimah's task is easy. The profound failure of efforts to arrive at a two-state solution is already clearly evident. Abunimah recalls that partition was first proposed by the British in the 1930s and then by the UN, before it evolved into what is more commonly referred to as the two-state solution. Both proposals are based on the idea that separating Arabs from Jews and dividing the land between them is the solution to the conflict, an idea that has been failing for more than seven decades.

> 'There is no workable partition,' he concludes, 'that is acceptable to a majority of Israelis and Palestinians.'

The alternative for Abunimah is a single state in historic Palestine, where

Israelis and Palestinians have equal rights. The borders between Israel and the occupied territories would be removed, uniting the land from the river to the sea. Jewish settlers would be able to remain in place, and Palestinian refugees would find their place in the new state, thus fulfilling their dream of returning to their homeland. Jerusalem would be the united capital of the new state.

At this point, Abunimah moves from a realistic demonstration of the hopelessness of the two-state solution, to an idealistic vision of a one-state solution. The moral basis of his advocacy is powerful. Equality, he says, demands that all the inhabitants of Palestine be able to participate in its political life, and have a say in who governs them. All those living on the land should have the right to vote, and the state should treat them equally without regard to religion, ethnicity or ideology.

Abunimah wants to overcome history. He insists it doesn't matter who has a historical right to be on the land and who doesn't. The battle of narratives need not be resolved to arrive at a just peace. It is enough to recognize the fact that both people inhabit the same land, and deserve the same universal rights.

Drawing heavily on the South African experience, Abunimah makes a comparison between the African National Congress and the Palestinian Liberation Organization. He lauds the former for transcending black nationalism and formulating an inclusive vision that appealed to whites, while criticizing the Palestinian leadership for its fixation on statehood and diplomatic recognition instead. According to the writer, it is a mixture of resistance to apartheid and the offer of an alternative to address Afrikaners' fears which ultimately convinced them to give up their hold on power and their ideology of racial separation. The Palestinians have yet to arrive at a similar formula.

Abunimah makes an impassioned plea to Palestinians and their supporters to construct a vision for the future that Israelis can be a part of. He says it is a matter of urgency for the Palestinians to provide a quick alternative to extreme ideas which are increasingly taking hold in Israel.

It would be unfair to interpret Abunimah's stress on the need for a Palestinian initiative as shifting responsibility from the Israelis to the Palestinians. A son of Palestinian refugees, Abunimah is personally aware of the destruction wrought on his people by the Zionist enterprise. His insistence on overcoming past bitterness is laudable not just for the human spirit it reflects, but also for the example it provides.

But can a vision, however well-articulated, overcome the raw balance of power, and persuade the Zionist state to give up its ideology and power?

While many Palestinians remain ambiguous about pursuing a one-state option, the Israelis are decidedly dead-set against it. As things stand, they already possess effective control of all of historic Palestine. International constraints occasionally restrain their more extreme impulses, but they have pushed ahead with settlement expansion in the West Bank largely unchecked.

Resistance, whether civil or military, does not appear to be having much effect on Israeli actions and attitudes, and neither does the international consensus against settlement expansion. To Abunimah, settlement expansion is just another nail in the coffin of the two-state delusion. The more geographically intertwined the two populations are, the harder it is to divide the land. However, there remains a missing link between the final demise of partition as a solution, and the desired emergence of a democratic state. One does not necessarily lead to the other, and perpetual conflict remains a possibility.

Abunimah successfully demonstrates the absurdity of sticking to the two-state approach, both on realistic and moral grounds. He also makes a disarming case for peace based on reconciliation and universal human rights. On the practical front, however, a lot more work is needed.

Ghadi Al-Hadi

Gore

Garrett G. Fagan, *The Lure of the Arena: Social Psychology and the Crowd at the Roman Games*, Cambridge University Press, 374 pages, paperback ISBN 9780521185967, £22.99

Faced with a book on the Holocaust, George Steiner expostulated, 'How in God's name do you review a book like this?' I felt the same about what Fagan (p. 79) rightly dubs 'a gruesome catalogue' and 'dismal litany'.

The Roman arena is well-trodden ground, as Fagan's 33-page bibliography shows: he seems to have read everything except Herbert Benario's pertinent article (*Classical Journal*, 1981) on amphitheatre crowd capacitiies, and (I unblushingly subjoin) my own cognate contribution (*Liverpool Classical Monthly*, 1984). Unlike Michael Grant (*The Gladiators*, 1970), who called them Nazis, Fagan recognises that the Romans had no monopoly on sadistic 'entertainments', surveying in horrific detail – this is an unavoidably stomach-turning read – similar atrocities from mediaeval times to Tyburn public hangings to (for example) North Korea where children are herded in to watch executions.

In Ernest Bramah's *Kai Lung's recapitulation*: 'Hanging, slicing, pressing, boiling, roasting, grilling, freezing, vatting, racking, twisting, drawing, compressing, inflating, rending, spiking, gouging, limb-tying, piecemeal pruning, and a variety of less tersely describable discomforts'.

One Roman justification was religious. Games were *munera*, a word designating obligations to the dead, Homeric and Etruscan (especially the latter: blaming the Etruscans for bad things in their own culture was a Roman speciality) antecedents being adduced, along with arena attendants and rituals got up in mythological style and representations (for example, dropping the failed aviator Icarus from high above). This extended into both pagan and Christian visions of eternal tortures in their respective hells. The secular excuse was that all arena victims – beast-fighters, gladiators, slaves, convicted criminals including Christians – were *infames* or *noxii*, guilty and so deserving their hideous fates.

When Nero burned Christians alive to illuminate an evening entertainment, Tacitus (*Annals* 15. 44) comments that they thoroughly deserved this – unlike the crowd which showed pity – a word for which (said the orator-imperial tutor Fronto) was lacking in Latin, as is an exact equivalent to our 'sport'. Again, not confined to 'pagan' Rome. Christian emperor Constantine's throwing of German prisoners to the lions was hailed by a contemporary orator as 'a deed lovelier than his triumph, for the pleasure of us all'.

The usually humane Samuel Johnson pronounced 'Executions are intended to draw spectators'. If they do not, they don't answer their purpose. The old method (namely, the just-banned public hangings) was most satisfactory to all parties; 'the publick was gratified by a procession; the criminal was supported by it'. Roman attitudes were mixed. Some emperors and intellectuals were openly disdainful. The ancient *Philogelos jokebook* (see my 1983 translation) makes fun of a crucified runner and other victims (nos. 121, 216, 217).

Fagan (pp. 241-245) enlarges on what he calls 'Disposition Theory', that is, crowds felt entitled to enjoy seeing the guilty suffer, his key to understanding the Roman attitude. There is something in this, though the darker side of human nature hardly needs dressing up in the socio-psychological jargon rampant in this book (living up or down to its sub-title), most of which I could have done without, albeit redeemed by some flashes of wit.

Fagan convincingly dismisses many other theories, including Aristotle's famous Catharsis (purgation of emotions). When he writes 'If anything, watching aggression and violence heightens aggressive impulses', I have to agree, having just watched the Vancouver ice-hockey riots.

Despite his prolix and repetitive style (never using one word where twenty will do), Fagan basically and rightly wields Occam's razor. Adducing the ever-increasing modern taste for violence in books, computer-games, films and so on (I recall the craze for 'snuff' movies, real or fake), he concludes that there have been, are, and always will be some people with depraved appetites, though one might switch gear and ask if there is really anything wrong with gladiatorial combats between consenting adults?

How many, though? Rome's population is usually estimated around one million. The Colosseum seated 54,760 spectators. The Circus Maximus was anciently said to accommodate 385,000. Even (as most do) scaling down the latter figure, we have the hopeful implication that far more people preferred the morally harmless chariot racing (though many enjoyed the frequent pile-ups, as at motor-car races) to arena slaughter. Hopkins and Beard (*The Colosseum*, 2005) come up with two surprising and welcome revelations: the death-rate among gladiators was only one in six, and in provincial arenas there were no more than two shows a year.

Fagan asks, how many of us would go to a revived Roman arena? That was always my question to undergraduate audiences, with the follow-up: how many would go twice?

Minutiae. Augustine's description of rectal fistula operations (*City of God* 22. 8) would have endorsed Fagan (pp. 31-32) on ancient pain endurance. Something (to redress the gender gap) might have been said on female arena performers, evidenced by (for example) Juvenal and Suetonius, excavations at Southwark, and an inscription in the British Museum. His attempt to poo-poo Marxist 'wishful thinking' (p. 171 + n. 48 – Geoffrey de St Croix is the target) is refuted by massive contrary evidence including the Pompeian graffito 'I hate the poor', quoted (p. 35) by himself – the Communist Manifesto's opening remains valid. Calpurnius Siculus (p. 119) is now commonly dated much later than Nero's time; cf. my article in *Illinois Classical Studies*, 1995. Martial's poem on the crucified Laureolus seems (p.181) misunderstood, Laureolus being the Beggar's Opera-like hero of a Roman stage mime. I noticed occasional trifling misprints ('ficiton', p. 16 n. 25; 'vicitims', p. 259), and one false reference (Pliny, NH 7. 168 should be 7. 186, p. 94 n. 35).

Skimpy index and mere handful of sometimes blurry monochrome illustrations are offset by rich appendix of Roman texts, with translations, including inscriptional evidences not always readily available elsewhere. For industry, meticulous documentation of primary and secondary sources, cosmic view, and a good dose of common sense throughout, this is now unquestionably the best book on this repulsive but unavoidable subject. To adapt a famous though possibly apocryphal gladiatorial chant, *Ave, Fagan Imperator! Lecturi Te Salutant!*

Barry Baldwin

The Most Honourable Spies

Paul Broda, *Scientist Spies: A memoir of my three parents and the atom bomb*, Matador, 344 pages, 2011, hardback ISBN 9781848766075, £17.50

It is widely supposed that blame for the 'Cold War' between the USA and USSR after 1945 could be laid at the door of the spies who gave the secrets of the atom bomb to the Soviets. A leading candidate for this accusation was the English physicist, Alan Nunn May, who was jailed for ten years for transgressing the Official Secrets Act. Rebecca West in a widely circulated book, *The Meaning of Treason,* made a quite remarkably unpleasant personal attack on Nunn May's character and judgement.

It so happens that Nunn May was a close friend of my wife and mine. It was always our view that his action, in so far as it really did help the Soviets to speed up their development of a nuclear bomb, ensured that the Cold War did not become a hot war. If the US had sole possession of nuclear weapons, it was clear they could use that power to dominate the world. They had already used the bomb twice in Japan, although the Japanese were already suing for an end to military activity. They could use it again, or the threat of its use, to win their way. With two in possession of such a weapon, there was mutually assured destruction, MAD in short. Mad it certainly was, but not likely to be risked, although in the Cuban crisis it seemed very likely.

So what is the importance of this new book by Paul Broda, himself the son and stepson, as he explains, of atomic scientist spies? The book is based on the letters of his father and a long memorandum from his stepfather. Both had knowledge of nuclear science which they shared with Soviet scientists, but the book clearly establishes that neither gained any financial advantage. Both acted in the belief that, at the time, the Soviet Union was an ally of the US and UK, and had been promised by Churchill and Roosevelt 'any technical or economic assistance that is in our power'.

Instead, the Soviet Union had been ruthlessly excluded from any knowledge of the development of a nuclear weapon, and anyone breaking this rule would be severely punished. Berti Broda was not convicted and sent to prison, as Nunn May was, but suffered as Nunn May did from being excluded from scientific posts, in Broda's case in Austria, which they both certainly merited.

Both Nunn May and Berti Broder were Communist Party members or sympathisers with the Soviet Union, Nunn May in England and Berti Broda in Austria. For a time during the war Berti and his wife, Hilda, and son, Paul, lived in England. After the war Berti returned to Austria, but Hilda and Paul stayed in England, and Hilda became divorced from Berti. She qualified as a doctor and worked in public health in Cambridge.

Nunn May had been a lodger before the war in the London flat of Eleanor Singer, who later became my wife, and Hilda had worked with Eleanor in hospitals in London, but there is no evidence that Nunn May and Hilda met until Nunn May came out of prison in 1953 and went to Cambridge. It was not, however, entirely a surprise to Eleanor and me, when Hilda and Alan came from Cambridge to see us to say that they were going to marry. After their wedding, they came to our house, to escape the journalists and thereafter we had several holidays with them, especially a long holiday in Dorset with our two children and their adopted son Johnny, before they went to work in Ghana. When, many years later, they came back again to England, we saw them and Paul on many occasions.

I tell all this story, which is told at great length in the book by Paul Broda, to establish my credentials for confirming what I regard as the quite honourable nature of Nunn May's spying. It can be argued against any testimony of my wife and myself that, in the 1940s and early 50s, we, too, were in the Communist Party. We left in 1956 over Hungary and Khrushchev's revelations, but the point at issue is our trust in Alan Nunn May. If you live with a couple as closely as we did with Alan and Hilda, you come to have a very clear understanding of what goes on in their minds and motivates them. I am of course aware that Nunn May broke his promise to obey the Official Secrets Act, but, after deep consideration and for reasons that he truly believed mattered for the survival of peoples' freedom and indeed of the very planet that we live on. The Nazi armies had not yet, in 1942, been defeated at Stalingrad, when Nunn May told what he knew. If you had known what he knew from his association in Canada with the secretive American development of the atom bomb, what would you have done?

In later years, Nunn May bitterly regretted that he had ever become involved in the development of what came to be a murderous weapon of war and of military domination. Once involved in it he had to be sure that the nuclear weapon was shared – and he paid the price for it in ten long years in prison and exclusion thereafter from all scientific employment in

Europe or North America. The British Government even tried to prevent Nkrumah employing him in the University of Accra in Ghana. Paul Broda has performed an important task in presenting this story, which only his personal involvement with the main characters, and his very considerable scientific knowledge as a UMIST professor, has made possible.

Michael Barratt Brown

Transcendentalism

Alan H. Batten, *Our Enigmatic Universe*, Melrose Books, 208 pages, ISBN 9781907732034, £8.99

The overarching theme of *Our Enigmatic Universe* is that science and religion have always maintained a complex relationship but that the two aren't necessarily mutually exclusive. For many centuries philosophers, scientists and religious scholars have expounded theories about why we are here, how we are here and what happens when we are no longer here. No one answer has satisfied all and even now, with all our technological advances in science and astronomy, there is no one unified theory of everything. The universe is an unimaginably complex and enigmatic place and because of this the author suggests that we do not have to take what is revealed to us through our senses as the only possible reality.

According to the blurb on the back of the book, 'the universe may have other aspects, termed "transcendent" in this book, partially revealed to us by the arts and music, so room can be found also for a religious dimension'. From the beginning, the author suggests that although we cannot perceive the entire universe because our senses are not equipped to view everything as it is in itself (the transcendent), some of us can see a little more than the rest, and this is where God sits – in the seat between what we know we can perceive and what we can't/don't know.

In Chapter Two he talks about birds navigating using magnetic fields and eels generating their own electric impulses; he suggests that we only understand these elements of our world because we have studied them but can't 'see' or sense them in the same way these animals do. To highlight his argument he presents the reader with a thought experiment:

'... let us imagine that intelligent beings could somehow evolve in the vicinity of a stellar X-ray source. The "eyes" of such beings would evolve to be most sensitive to that part of the electromagnetic spectrum which was most intense in the radiation from their "sun" – i.e. the X-rays. The most conspicuous objects in the night-time sky would be other X-ray stars. What we call "normal stars" would be invisible to the astronomers of that planet, at best, some of the nearest ones, emitting weak X-rays, might appear as very "faint" objects.' (p. 20)

It is here that he begins to make his case for the theme that runs through the book. As *homo sapiens* we might not be able to 'know' all of the universe – we will see only what our senses allow us to detect and the sense data we receive from this observation will be processed in a uniquely 'human' way – but we can 'infer' from what we do know that which we don't. From this he extrapolates that all phenomena that cannot be wholly known in a scientific way will fall into the category of that which lies just outside of human perception; phenomena can be said to exist, it's just that we cannot 'see' them.

Batten discusses many philosophers in his well-researched book but it is specifically his reference to Kant and the transcendent that caught my attention. As Kant writes in his hefty tome *The Critique of Pure Reason*, we perceive the world not as 'it is in itself' but as it appears to us. This doctrine of Transcendental Idealism asserts that human beings necessarily perceive objects as located in time and space. However, space and time do not exist as a part of the object because space and time provide only the 'backdrop' to the objects being perceived. In other words, objects exist *in* space and time, but space and time are not a part of an object as it is in itself.

A way of understanding this aspect of Kant's theory is to imagine a theatre auditorium. The audience (of one) is the observer, the set on stage represents the objects being observed, and backstage is space and time wherein all the objects exist as they are in themselves and not as they appear to us. This way of expressing Kant's theory is not to be confused with Plato's cave. The objects on stage in this analogy don't exist elsewhere (as they do for Plato); it is just that the observer is making sense of the atoms that come together to form an object against the backdrop of space and time.

Nowhere in his doctrine of Transcendental Idealism does Kant invoke divine intervention; yet, if I have understood correctly the assertions made in *Our Enigmatic Universe*, Batten is suggesting that it is a rational assumption that God is sitting backstage designing the set for all his observers. And, in Chapter Four, Batten does consider the arguments from intelligent design and concludes that they 'can help show that it is not totally irrational to believe in God, but they fall short of being conclusive proof' (p.74).

In his compact book, Batten tries to marry up the scientific and the philosophical with the religious dimension of our understanding of the universe. Whilst he delivers many complex philosophical, scientific and religious concepts in a succinct and digestible fashion, some of the subjects need further expansion in order for them to be joined in an enduring partnership.

Abi Rhodes